The Art of Activism and the Activism of Art

First published in 2022 by Lund Humphries

Lund Humphries
Huckletree Shoreditch
Alphabeta Building
1 Finsbury Square
London EC2A 1AH
UK

www.lundhumphries.com

ISBN 978-1-84822-441-4
eBook (Mobi) 978-1-84822-443-8
eBook (ePub) 978-1-84822-444-5
eBook (pdf) 978-1-84822-442-1

A Cataloguing-in-Publication record for this book is available from the British Library

Copy edited by Clare Farrow
Designed by Wolfe Hall
Set in Mediaan by Dávid Molnár
and WH Aldine Mono by Wolfe Hall
Printed by Tallinna Raamatutrükikoda, Estonia

The Art of Activism and the Activism of Art

Gregory Sholette

LUND HUMPHRIES

7 Foreword by Marcus Verhagen

9 *Chapter 1*
The Contemporary Artist as Activist:
This is Not Just a Test

21 *Chapter 2*
The Situationists' Total Critique,
and Total Cure

32 *Chapter 3*
Grupo de Artistas de Vanguardia

39 *Chapter 4*
Escaping the Long Greenbergian Shadow

48 *Chapter 5*
1968 and After: The Phantom Archive
of Social-Movement Culture

59 *Chapter 6*
1970s: The Activist Turn in Art

71 *Chapter 7*
1980s: Artists respond to the
Neoliberal Turn

86 *Chapter 8*
1990s: Repurposing Situationism
as Tactical Media

98 *Chapter 9*
Back to the Streets: From Tactical Media
to Occupy Wall Street (2011)

106 *Chapter 10*
Institutional Critique or Cultural Abolition?

116 *Chapter 11*
2016 and After: Winter Is Coming/
Winter Is Here

132 *Chapter 12*
Black Lives Matter: Fugitivity in Plain Sight

139 *Chapter 13*
The Contemporary Artist as Activist:
Conjectures, Hauntologies and
Inconclusions

152 Notes

166 Appreciation

167 Further reading and archives

169 Image credits

170 Index

NEW DIRECTIONS IN CONTEMPORARY ART

Series Editor: Marcus Verhagen, Senior Lecturer, Sotheby's Institute of Art, London

A series of newly commissioned, engaging, critical texts identifying key topics and trends in contemporary art practice and discussing their impact on the wider art world and beyond. The art world is changing rapidly as artists avail themselves of new technologies, travel ever more widely, reach out to new audiences and tackle urgent issues, from climate change to mass migration. The purpose of the series is to discuss these and other changes, in texts that are accessible, stimulating and polemical.

INTERNATIONAL SERIES ADVISORY BOARD

Foreword

The early 21st century has been an extraordinary period for art activism, with movements from Occupy to Black Lives Matter drawing on the artistic skills of adherents. As Gregory Sholette argues in these pages, we have not seen a period of such vitality in protest culture since the 1960s and 70s. Activists have toppled monuments, in some cases replacing them with new memorials. Widespread efforts have been made, by groups such as Decolonise This Place, to hold art institutions to account for art-washing and for perpetuating discriminatory practices and narratives. We have also in recent years seen the rise of collectives like Forensic Architecture, which operates at the intersection of art, forensic science and activism, the Center for Political Beauty, which has organised provocative events targeting the German far right and the treatment of refugees, and The Unbribables, which has launched actions highlighting corruption in Serbia.

This book tells the story of these and other art activists, their means, objectives and trajectories. Some are artists engaged in activism, others activists who have turned their hands to art. Sholette examines their activities from the perspective of an artist and activist who has been active in the field since the 1980s. His own involvement in some activist groups and proximity to others are crucial to the breadth and depth of a study that is grounded in what he calls 'the phantom archive', that is to say, in the vast array of materials, with their underlying codes, that have been fashioned by art activists but largely omitted from the art historical record. The methodological thrust of this text is in keeping with its topic: it is a bottom-up account.

Sholette's longstanding involvement also allows him to trace breaks and continuities in the historical evolution of art activism.

And his book offers not just a cultural history of activism but also a parallel intellectual history, examining the texts and ideas that have inspired activist art, some of which continue to reverberate long after their historical moment, like those of the Situationists, which still serve as touchstones for activists today. Sholette is keen to stress the uses of history, its practical repercussions for the activism of the present.

At times in this book he is fiercely hopeful, as he is for instance in his perception of the progressive dissolution of the distinction between art and activism. At other times his writing is pessimistic. Certainly, he puts forward a grim assessment of the recent evolution of the art world. It is rare to read a book in which notes of hope and pessimism dovetail as tightly and jarringly as they do here – and in this too Sholette's text reproduces something of the structure of his chosen topic.

Marcus Verhagen

Chapter 1

The Contemporary Artist as Activist: *This is Not Just a Test*

'Maybe the Trojan Horse was the first activist artwork. Based in subversion on the one hand and empowerment on the other, activist art operates both within and beyond the beleaguered fortress that is high culture or the "art world".'[1]
Lucy R. Lippard

'The artistic imagination continues to dream of historical agency.'[2]
Martha Rosler

'Take the Quiz', prompts the canny pop-up questionnaire on the Tate's website (fig.21). 'Which art collective do you belong to?'[3] 'Should you be in the *Black Audio Film Collective* ... or are you a *Hackney Flasher* at heart?' The test refers to a pair of London-based artist groups from the 1970s and 1980s, one focused on the British African diaspora, the other on working women's rights. More questions immediately follow: 'Who makes up your collective? What is your mission all about? What inspires you?' Click, click, click, and the platform's algorithm reveals your innermost communal proclivities (somehow, I wound up belonging to a group of early-19th-century painters known as the Ancients who gathered at the home of the poet William Blake). Scrolling down, the page offers information about how to 'start a movement' and short biographies of other 'radical art

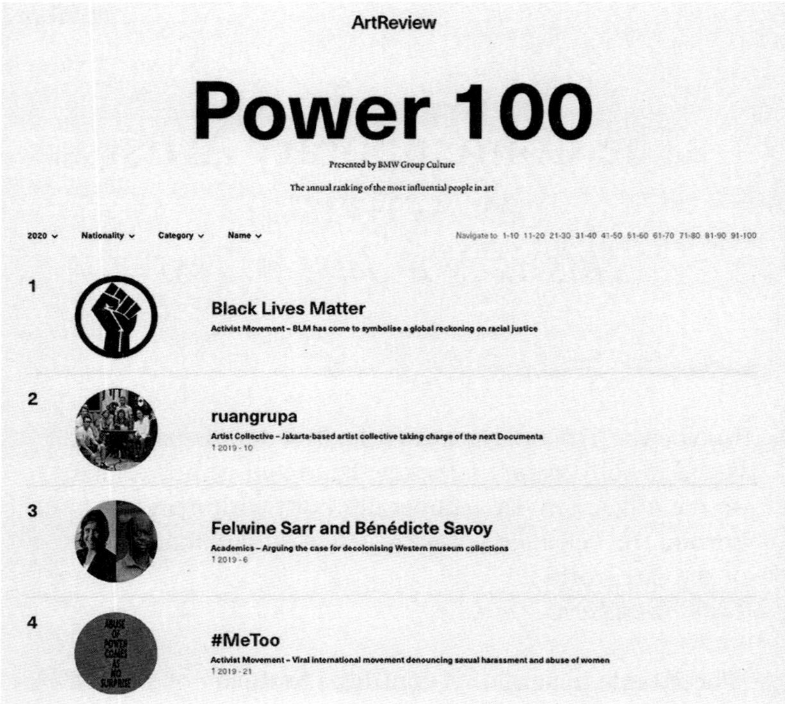

Fig.1 The most influential people in the 2020 annual art ranking by *ArtReview* magazine, online graphics. Screen shot @gsholette (Twitter), 3 December 2020

groups', as well as a large button that leads to a £5 membership deal for discounted tickets and 29 per cent off café items, all puckishly marketed under the brand name 'Tate Collective'.

The fact that an institutional pillar of contemporary global high culture such as the Tate is endorsing, however waggishly, collectives and activist art, signals a marked change towards overtly political and socialized practices. Once omitted from standard art historical accounts and museum collections, artistic activism and collectivism is now visible virtually everywhere in the art world and beyond. How should we understand this development? Consider that about one year after the Tate created this webpage, more than a hundred of the museum's employees staged a labor strike in protest of 'pandemic-related' job cuts. The ax was initially falling on half the workforce, but specifically the most precarious staff members, even as senior administrators continued earning six-figure salaries. The truth is that most, if not all, of the 'radical art groups' listed on the Tate's site would, if they were still around, be marching outside the museum on the picket line, thus hypothetically leaving the museum's webpage empty of content. The meaning, and possible consequences of these tensions, contradictions and historical forgetting, is one of several key themes that this brief book seeks to address.

ACTIVIST ART REDUX

We are witnessing today a surge of artistic activism unlike anything since the 1960s and 1970s. Recent museum interventions, exhibition boycotts, picket lines, occupations, mocking mimetic websites and staff unionization campaigns target unfair labor practices, institutional racism, colonial collections and financial ties between museum board members and weapons manufacturers, fossil fuel extractors, opioid producers and real estate speculators. Just as emphatic is the surge of artistic activism taking place 'outside' the art world's institutional boundaries, including performative street protests employing stencils, banners, graphics, puppets, protest pageantry and makeshift counter-memorials in city streets. From Ferguson, Missouri, to London, Cali, Hong Kong, Kyiv, Moscow and Palestine, a spectacular protest aesthetic is present everywhere in plain sight. Meanwhile, monuments commemorating white supremacy and colonialism are defaced, demolished and tagged with the names of Black, brown and poor citizens murdered by the police and military. In São Paulo, an art group called Peripheral Revolution (Revolução Periférica) directly set alight a statue of Borba Gato, an 18th-century colonial exploiter of Brazil's land and people. In short, images of visual confrontation and creative dissent are impossible to avoid today; the very air seems electrified with what might be termed an art of activism, and its public facing appearance complements the activism of art taking place within the sphere of high culture.

On one level, activist art is a singular facet of the broader, accelerating field of socially engaged, collective and participatory art, a cultural phenomenon that also goes by such names as new genre, participatory, relational, dialogical aesthetics, and social practice art.[4] In a little over a decade, all these modes have moved from the margins of the art world to a more central visibility. With this shift comes growing scrutiny and interest from younger artists, critics, theorists, historians and teachers, but also from NGOs, foundations and governmental policy makers, as well as a few commercial galleries and collectors. Without question, the prevailing desire by artists to transform their practices into a form of highly focused protest is the most prominent – and in many ways the most perplexing – constituent of contemporary art today. Indeed, activist art is a far stranger phenomenon than it might at first appear.

What precisely defines the contemporary activist artist? As opposed to only representing politics or social injustice, the activist artist can be distinguished by an unyielding focus on agitation and protest as an artistic medium. Typically, these practitioners operate collectively, working with other artists, but also in collaboration with 'non-art' political activists, and on occasion they do manage to bring about a degree of positive societal change as we shall see. Sometimes this activist engagement is carried out subtly, although more frequently, and especially recently, it employs a degree of militancy that makes artistic practice appear barely distinguishable from activism per se. It is this increasingly tenuous line – if a line still exists at all – between the practices of the artist as activist and the activist as such, that is another primary concern of this book. For if the indeterminate boundary between cultural practice and political activism has been breached, then the repercussions for both art and politics are significant. And if, as Martha Rosler proposes (see opening quote), the artistic imaginary has long dreamt of its own historical agency, then it seems that in the second decade of the 21st century, it is historical agency itself that now dreams of its own aesthetic incarnation.

THE ARTIST AS ACTIVIST, THEN AND NOW

As early as 1934, Walter Benjamin explicitly called upon all progressive writers, artists and intellectuals to produce their work tendentiously: by challenging traditional methods of reportage, photographic representation and audience reception, as well as by explicitly advocating for the proletarian struggle against fascism and in favor of the cause of socialism.[5] Benjamin's frequently cited essay 'The Author as Producer' builds upon a long history in which artists were tasked with representing a changing roster of agendas: philosophical, religious, revolutionary and pro-state oriented. More than a hundred years before Benjamin wrote his treatise, the French philosopher Henri de Saint-Simon insisted that artists are the advanced forces of a new society, right alongside scientists and industrialists, arguing that this 'is the duty of artists, this is their mission.'[6] On the eve of the Bolshevik Revolution, Vladimir Lenin determined that culture must serve the 'politically-conscious vanguard of the entire working class.'[7] Thousands of years before either Lenin or Saint-Simon, Plato sought to expel artists and poets, including the beloved Homer, from the ideal Greek republic on charges of merely imitating reality. But those artists who honored the state's national heroes could remain. And closer to our own time, the early 1980s New York-based artist collective Political Art Documentation /Distribution (PAD/D), to which I once belonged, flatly insisted that the group 'cannot serve as a means of advancement within the art world structure of museums and galleries. Rather, we have to develop new forms of distribution economy as well as art.' Our ultimate goal was to use our artistic skills to support radical and decolonial liberation movements around the world.[8]

This was certainly a tall order for a small collective of artists relatively marginalized from the cultural mainstream. Furthermore, PAD/D's mission statement was printed on newsprint using inexpensive offset press technology and distributed by hand within art galleries, cafes and through the postal system. Crucially, the most recent wave of artistic activism is no longer limited to ink, paper and mail carriers, any more than it is restricted to fixed moments in real time or specific spaces of action. Thanks to the immediacy and fungibility of online, digital and cellular communications networks, political interventions can now migrate immediately into an electronic ether, sometimes even originating online as memes, tweets, BreadTube videos, fake museum websites all situated alongside comical 60-second TikTok housecat escapades and a plethora of visually alluring Instagram posts. Once this cyber-activist imagery is uploaded, a swarm of participants can re-edit and redistribute new versions that essentially over-write the original. In short, the medium of protest aesthetics has certainly expanded, but whether its objectives have changed is a question taken up in the chapters ahead.

OCCUPY NFTS, DON'T JUST MINT THEM

Redeploying, repurposing and reactivating imagery and other content is today central to contemporary art activism, which appears to draw upon a vast, almost spectral archive of available sources for its exposition. By contrast, the emergence of non-fungible tokens, or NFTs, introduces a seemingly baffling reversal of this repurposing aesthetic by freezing the infinite reproducibility of the digital medium within a unique and un-hackable blockchain ledger that underwrites the work's provenance, originality and authorship. And yet this same encrypted guarantee subverts the radical interchangeability (fungibility) of the digital medium itself. Perhaps that is good news for some, including under-represented artists, and more power to them; however, with auction sales skyrocketing for NFTs, why is it that capitalist monetization always comes out on top at the end of the day? There is also this caveat, that artists Dread Scott and Hito Steyerl have recently used blockchain technology to generate critically engaging activist interventions that turn the NFT phenomenon on its head: Scott by 'auctioning off' a white person's enslaved image at Christie's in New York (fig.2), and Steyerl by turning the Royal Academy of Art in London into a blockchain piece, which she donated to the school's students in exchange for re-envisioning their institution as a communal cooperative.[9]

THE REVOLUTION THIS TIME

Speculations regarding emancipation through technological innovation will return in Chapter 8, but for now, it is inarguable that scores of younger artists today seek to challenge the political and economic shortcomings of the institutional art world, even if few directly interact with its global topography or benefit from its multi-billion-dollar marketplace, and fewer still know much about the backstory of activist art. Consider this personal anecdote from a little over a decade ago as one barometer for the speed and intensity of this shift. In 2008, the MIT journal *October* invited me and a large group of artists, theorists and writers to reflect on the cultural sector's tepid response to the 2003 US-led invasion of Iraq under President George W. Bush, which UN Secretary-General Kofi Annan condemned as illegal.[10] My contribution began with a negative historical comparison, pointing out that reactions by artists and academics to similarly atrocious public events were once far more direct and confrontational, decades earlier. I then rattled

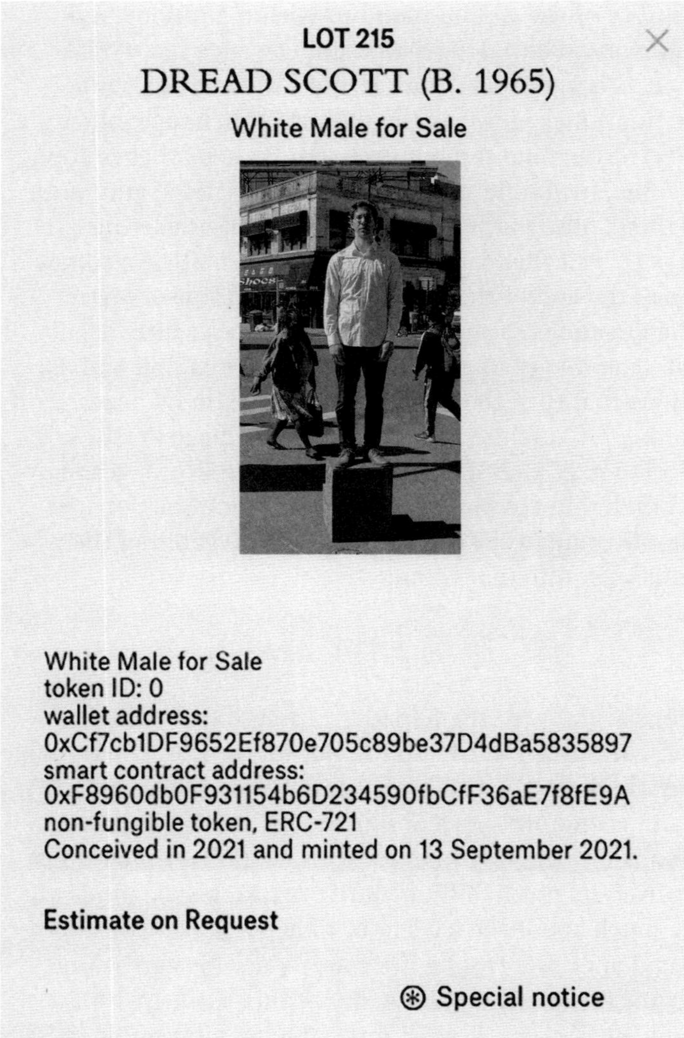

Fig.2 Christie's auction page for Dread Scott's NFT project *White Male for Sale*, 1 October 2021

off examples, such as in 1970, when the Art Workers' Coalition and its faction Guerrilla Art Action Group staged a fake gun battle on the street in front of the Museum of Modern Art to protest against the war in Vietnam, or in the mid-1980s, when a broad coalition titled Artists' Call Against US Intervention in Central America organized an omnibus series of exhibitions and events that took place in alternative spaces as well as commercial galleries, with a poster designed by Claes Oldenburg to oppose a seemingly imminent invasion of El Salvador by the Reagan Administration. My essay concluded despairingly by insisting that activist art was a thing of the past: 'militant street theater, interventionist scholarship, activist curating, artists directly challenging their own well-being by denouncing museums and the art market ... all of this appears inconceivable today,' I wrote.[11]

Nothing could be further from our current reality. Indeed, I would never have predicted that in 2020, the activist group Black Lives Matter (BLM) would be selected to top the annual ranking of 100 art world influencers by a leading industry journal, with the #MeToo movement close behind in fourth place (fig.1).[12] The perceived influence of BLM and #MeToo on high culture underscores the ascendency of activist aesthetics within the mainstream art world. Likewise, the coveted Turner Prize was awarded in 2021 to the Belfast-based Array Collective who transformed an unlicensed Northern Ireland pub into 'a place to gather outside entrenched Sectarian divides.'[13] I could also cite a few dozen books that have appeared in recent years, or are about to be published, that drive home the point, including studies of the socially-engaged practitioners Tania Bruguera, Zanele Muholi, Ai Weiwei, Pussy Riot, as well as the hilariously illustrated and drolly smart workbook by the Center for Art Activism entitled *The Art of Activism: Your All-Purpose Guide to Making the Impossible Possible*, from OR Books.[14]

Activist art has undergone such a rapid rise in stature that the curator Peter Weibel suggests it 'may be the first new art form of the twenty-first century', while cultural theorist Boris Groys insists that art activism is an entirely 'new phenomenon'.[15]

Contrarily, I will show that it is possible to construct a credible backstory for art activism, one that stretches back decades, if not centuries should we wish to consider the elaborate floats that Jacques-Louis David designed for public *fêtes* to rally support for the French Revolution in the 1790s, or Gustave Courbet's decisive role in the toppling of the Vendôme Column during the Paris Commune. Nonetheless, for reasons of practicality and conciseness, I concentrate in this short study on activist art from the 1960s to early 2022. Even so, examples are so numerous that the chapters to come offer merely a selection of this wildly branching genealogy. Furthermore, the book does not add up to anything resembling a proper linear art history, for any attempt to historicize art activism must recognize it is a phenomenon with no singular manifesto or specified aesthetic protocols, that gives rise to no official school or accepted canon. Neither is activist art systematically collected or exhibited, although a few specialized archival collections have significant holdings.[16] It would be more accurate to suggest that whatever chronological record activist art offers, it appears at best to be a fragmented and boisterous reservoir of past interventions, experiments, repetitions and compromises, as well as minor victories and outright failures. I will refer to this alternately as a surplus or phantom archive whose accessibility calls for speculative processes of reclamation, repurposing and reactivation, as opposed to more customary art historical methods involving the formal, iconographic or biographical attributes of an artwork, movement or artist. To cite queer feminist theorist Tirza True Latimer, when it comes to subjects characterized by a pattern of historical invisibility and erasure, one must sometimes mobilize 'techniques frowned on by 'proper historians ... ' by viewing 'gaps, absences, and apparitions as historically consequential.'[17] Reading Latimer in conjunction with Antonio Gramsci's observation that history leaves behind an infinity of traces, but without providing an inventory, I would say that the archival terrain of this study is as real as it is indeterminate, but is always stretching towards a seemingly unattainable encounter with its own missing inventory.[18]

Think of this book, therefore, as akin to a particle accelerator: a device for uncovering and measuring concrete, material things that elude immediate detection, things that nevertheless remain indispensable to the very nature of reality, or in this instance, to the reality of contemporary art. Along with asking why activist art is gaining renewed visibility and whether it still remains distinct from non-art political activism, this accelerator apparatus also probes a certain dark matter creativity: the majority of imaginative and artistic labor that's long been closeted within mainstream art history. Like a shadow agency, this dark matter labor is made up of the many collectively generated projects, amateur practices and oppositional provocations typically relegated to the margins of the mainstream, even though its accumulated gravitational inertia paradoxically anchors the lofty summits of high culture.[19] Which is why some of the case studies to follow seemingly violate my own description of activist art as direct and confrontational. Under certain geopolitical circumstances, engaged art practices can, like Lippard's Trojan Horse, transform what would be merely a charming street mural of flowers and butterflies, or certain banned colors, into an act of transgression in places such as Afghanistan, Syria, Egypt, Hong Kong, Belarus and Ukraine.

My hope for this concise introduction is that it will provide readers not only with select details about activist art's postwar backstory, but also offer one or more sets of criteria for critically interpreting this phenomenon, as well as perhaps even reactivating its promised social and political agency. And while activist art may appear unique to present day circumstances as Weibel and Groys propose, like all cultural phenomena it is shaped by previous events and practices, even when practitioners borrow unknowingly from, or repurpose, its archival resources. As historian of socially engaged art Larne Abse Gogarty puts it, 'older forms resonate and make new meaning in the present', thus offering a potentially dynamic, 'usable past'.[20] For this reason, as much as my account is descriptive, and hopefully heuristic, it also seeks to accomplish something less conventional – let's call it the summoning of that which haunts the very paradigm of the artist as activist, and the art of activism in its most contemporary manifestation. And what is summoned must be confronted; its stipulations and effects acknowledged, weighed and at times deferred to.

Consequently, over the course of this terse excursion, we catch glimpses of an uneven yet persistent oppositional agency *from below* that continuously struggles for visibility, if not self-realization, most often in response to oppressive social conditions; only to submerge once again out of sight, until it doesn't, or until it won't. And this is the circumstance that I believe we have arrived at today: the emergence of a vigorous protest aesthetic, unfolding in a permanently aestheticized state of reality, or perhaps more accurately, in a state of social and political *unreality* brought about by the ultra-spectacularized conditions of 21st-century capitalism. My study begins therefore, with the loose-knit group of writers, thinkers and artists who made up the influential activist alliance known as the Situationist International (SI) (1957–72). They were not the first to theorize a certain form of capitalist aestheticization engendered by consumerism and mass media, but the SI generated the most succinct and influential interpretation of this phenomenon, whose effect threads its way throughout my entire treatise.

One final note before proceeding: please know that I was a founding and active member of the groups Political Art Documentation/Distribution, REPOhistory and Gulf Labor Coalition, all collectives that in full disclosure I will discuss over the course of this book.

The Situationists' Total Critique, and Total Cure

> 'In 1967, in a book entitled *The Society of the Spectacle,* I showed what the modern spectacle was already in essence: the autocratic reign of the market economy.'[1]
> *Guy Debord*

A great deal has been written about the Situationist International (SI) by scholars far more informed than I am on the subject. Still, even a short introductory book about the artist as activist must account for the group's enduring if uneven influence. I'd like to focus on three critical aspects of their work: the SI's analysis of capitalist aesthetics as a totalizing spectacle, the group's direct engagement with the radical student and worker uprisings of Paris in May 1968, and the ongoing, though inconsistent, legacy of the SI following the defeat of the New Left's revolutionary objectives in 1968. In this sense, the SI's project has been described as one, if not the last, stand for the historical avant-garde's ambition of completely transforming society from, top to bottom.[2]

TOTAL CRITIQUE OF THE TOTAL SOCIAL SPECTACLE

For some 15 years between 1957 and 1972, the artists, activists and theorists of the internationally-based SI organization engaged in a high-energy series of debates that sought to reconcile aspects of the radical artistic avant-garde with the

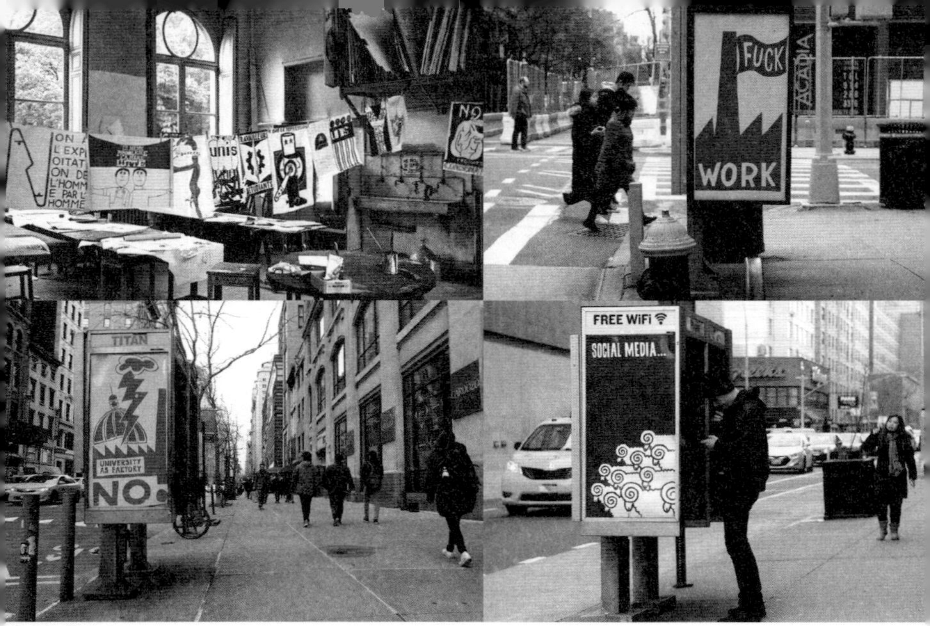

Fig.3 Josh MacPhee's 2019 tribute to the agitational street posters of the May 1968 Atelier Populaire in Paris (upper left), now focused on issues of electronic surveillance and capitalist privatization. Images placed on NYC streets by Art in Ad Places.

political avant-garde, all the while pivoting on a foundation of anti-authoritarian, libertarian communism. According to cultural theorist Sadie Plant, the SI was crucial to the Western European New Left intelligentsia because it introduced, or perhaps reintroduced:

> the radical demands of the imagination, creativity, desire, and pleasure to their revolutionary project, thus not only rejecting orthodox Marxist theory at the time, but also drawing on the legacy of Dada and Surrealism, whose provocative style, demands for immediacy, and cravings for autonomy were carried into the situationist project.[3]

The SI's liberatory aspiration also invoked the unbridled communist agency of Karl Marx's postcapitalist citizen, who defies imposed divisions of labor by hunting in the morning, fishing in the afternoon and doing critical theory in the evening, without ever becoming fisherman, hunter or critic (or artist, for that matter).[4] Indeed, in one form or another, the desire to be emancipated through the total liberation of human creativity is an idea that winds its way through the avant-garde's historical narrative, both before and after the SI, though seldom with such fervor. It also helps to explain the link between, say, 1920s French Surrealism, and Suzanne and Aimé Césaire's Afro-Surrealist, anticolonial movement on the French island of Martinique two decades later, as well as the SI's own engagement with Algerian freedom fighters 20 years after that. The proposed remedy for a completely commodified, alienating reality is complete decommodification, and a universal end to all forms of oppression – a solution as grand in scope as the depth of the ailment is itself.

The group's best-known theorist, Guy Debord, understood postindustrial capitalism as a force that was quickly evolving into an all-inclusive project intent on colonizing human consciousness, using what the Situationist's labeled the 'spectacular industries': television, film and publishing.[5] And while this process may have originated in the West, it was fast becoming a global force. In Europe and the US, the spectacle of commodity culture foisted a nearly involuntary consumerism on alienated workers in the form of an endless parade of gadgets, advertisements and other distractions. In the socialist nations, it took the form of authoritarian personality cults. According to Debord, it was the sociologist who maintained the logic of the spectacle in the West, and it was the police who progenerated it in the East.[6] At the end of the day, both forms of governance – Western privatized capitalism and what the SI considered merely a centralized, state-controlled version of capitalism in the USSR – orchestrated mass forms of public pageantry to assure uninterrupted productivity and consumption, as well as to gain control over leisure time and even infiltrate human desire itself.

What is significant about this analysis is its adherence to the Marxist category of totality, in which capitalism gradually subsumes all other aspects of social organization, agency and production under itself. Although this so-called 'grand narrative' approach to political and historical analysis was already disputed by poststructuralist and feminist theorists at the time, the SI maintained in 1963 that 'the coherence of this society cannot be understood without an all-encompassing critique, illuminated by the inverse project of a liberated creativity.'[7] This theorem remains persuasive for two reasons. First, the SI emphasizes the system's objective of absolute management over the human sensorium, including visual perception, vocalization and bodies inhabiting or moving through architecture, but also the cognitive and affective dimensions of both conscious and unconscious experience. Think of it as an aesthetic program particular to advanced capitalism, and here I am referring to *aisthētikos,* the ancient Greek word for sensory perception, and not solely the more familiar idea of aesthetics as beauty. Second, the only apparent solution to this dire condition is its utter inversion via 'liberated creativity', thus an aesthetic of truly emancipated imagination versus the pseudo-emancipatory aesthetic of consumerism under capital. In this regard, Jacques Rancière's influential idea of 'the distribution of the sensible' is an elaboration of the SI's analysis, although it introduces something very much at variance to the SI's fundamental thesis.[8]

Like other consequential theorists today, Rancière posits resistance and oppositionality as strictly localized ruptures or folds within the spectacle itself, a thesis that is perhpas only conceivable as political compensation in the aftermath of the failed revolution of 1968. It is in these darkened fissures and gaps (though strictly speaking we are not talking about specific places) that those who are not permitted to speak or who are forbidden their own visibility – either figuratively, sensually or as embodied beings—come to represent the system's limit as its negation. The task of regulating the risk that these resistant margins pose to the established social order falls to the 'police', Rancière's overarching term for juridical rules and conventions of inclusion and exclusion. We will return to questions of visibility and embodiment again, especially in Chapter 11, but I remind readers that for the SI, as much as for Rancière, Michel Foucault and others who derived important parts of their theory from the Situationists, the social sciences, mass education, racism and other disciplinary regimes are as much 'the police' as are the actual, uniformed *gendarmerie*.

The postmodern version of oppositionality is myriad in form and disarticulated in principle, meaning that no one social subject constitutes *the* anointed revolutionary force, as was the case for example with the proletariat for Marx and Engels. It is important to underscore that the SI held fast to the Marxian faith in working-class resistance to capitalism, even if they focused on radically autonomous organizing by workers, including anti-colonial revolutionaries, taking place outside official trade unions and established Communist and Trotskyist parties. This became especially evident during the feverish days of May 1968, discussed below. At the same time, the SI confronted the totalizing advance of spectacular capitalism with an equally total, although completely inverted, concept of counter-spectacle, in which everyday autonomous working people would gain 'control of all levels of their own history'.[9] Nonetheless, for the SI, unleashing this liberatory proletarian imagination and the historical potential submerged within it did not involve simply disconnecting from the spectacle, if that was even possible, or ignoring its fantastic optics. After all, Debord acknowledged that 'capitalism could appropriate even the most radical ideas and return them safely in the form of harmless ideologies'. Perhaps begrudgingly, therefore, he understood the significant role that aesthetic processes play in establishing the centrality of desire in the everyday experience of workers under capitalism.[10] To reject the spectacle would consequently require a method of freeing that which was held hostage by it, the imagination itself. The SI invented a two-step process of first appropriating and then subverting, or hijacking, the power of our own desires, which the aestheticized regime of the spectacular consumerism employs against us.

The group's term for this double procedure was '*détournement*', a blatant, politicized hustle in which mass-produced books, commercial artwork, movies, advertisements, billboards, cartoon strips and even maps were seized upon and redirected to work against their mercantile intentions. In 1956, the 8 May issue of the Belgian Surrealist magazine *Les Lèvres Nues* first announced the discovery of *détournement,* and the journal's cover illustrated this new avant-garde practice. What it shows is at first familiar: a schematic black and white map of France. On closer inspection, we see that all the major cities of the Gaullist République are intentionally mislabeled using place-names from the break-away French colony of Algeria. Thus, El Mesran instead of Bordeaux, Médéa rather than Nantes, and Algiers in place of Paris. A work of geographical *détournement,* the magazine cover expressed solidarity with the liberatory aims of the Algerian resistance who had declared independence from France two years earlier. The subversive graphic illustration typifies the *détournement* aesthetic, which filmmaker Jeffrey Skoller succinctly describes as simultaneously negating and revitalizing an existing image, or text, which is 'appropriated and transformed into something new and relevant to the current political moment'.[11]

The two societal groups strategically positioned to carry out these hijacking tactics were artists and students: artists because they belonged to the same sector of workers compelled to produce the spectacle in the first place, and were therefore also the most knowledgeable about its technical composition and inherent weaknesses; and students because they were the germinating product of capitalist society, 'just like Godard or Coca-Cola', but whose plasticity was still capable of being turned against the spectacle.[12] It was the convergence of artists and militant students with other workers in the streets of Paris in 1968, two years after those words were published, that continues to define the consequential role played by the SI for any artist seeking to become an activist today (fig.3).

MAY 1968

SI theory met historical circumstances head-on in the spring of 1968, when widespread student and worker rebellions broke out in a Parisian suburb before spreading across the city and then across France, arousing and building on similar unrest around the globe. In West Berlin, Chicago, Mexico City, Rio de Janeiro and Tokyo, among other cities, these audacious and escalating events were described by the theorist Herbert Marcuse as a 'Great Refusal', a protest 'against that which is', and Marcuse's model for such total negation was nothing less than art.[13] Notably, these nonconformist uprisings targeted mainstream governments as well as traditional leftist parties and trade unions. Sadie Plant affirms that the SI frequently turned its critical technique of *détournement* and liberated creativity against any group that represented orthodox cultural, political or economic theories, including the French Communist Party.

Student-led, anti-government protests also broke out in the socialist cities of Warsaw, Belgrade and Prague, the latter rebellion leading to a Soviet military intervention that brutally suppressed Czechoslovakia's brief promise of 'socialism with a human face'.[14] Meanwhile, police in the US violently attacked unarmed protestors who demanded an end to the war in

Vietnam at the Democratic National Convention in Chicago, while Mexican soldiers shot and murdered an unknown number of demonstrators in Mexico City's Tlatelolco neighborhood. But it was in Paris that the revolutionary spirit of the 1960s climaxed, with the near collapse of the postwar de Gaulle government. Art and activism converged via incendiary anti-capitalist posters, Molotov cocktails and improvised paving-stone barricades that harkened back to the Paris Commune of 1871. For about seven weeks, this counter-spectacle distracted public and media attention away from the city's array of hyperbolic billboards advertising sports cars, men's and women's fashions, and *le détergent glouton*, a popular laundry detergent whose sensationalized advertising campaign promised to arm housewives with an insurgent army of 'gluttonous' dirt-eating enzymes.

French students started occupying their universities, demanding educational reforms; soon after, they demanded an end to capitalism, and then to work itself. The 'Great Refusal' had begun. Following an initial police crackdown, millions of unionized factory workers staged a general strike in solidarity with the students, as the nation's economy came to a standstill. Leftist art students at the École des Beaux-Arts established a fast-turnaround screen-printing workshop, the Atelier Populaire, where bold, collectively produced images of factories flying red flags and unified worker silhouettes mixed with slogans such as 'Nous sommes le pouvoir' (We are the power) and 'La beauté est dans la rue' (Beauty is in the street). Undoubtedly, the Marxist-oriented art students of the Atelier Populaire had read and absorbed dissident Situationist theory, including the widely circulated 1966 pamphlet *On the Poverty of Student Life*, published by the SI in collaboration with students at the University of Strasbourg. Its concluding recommendation declares that 'the rules are simple: to live instead of devising a lingering death, and to indulge untrammelled desire'.[15]

The SI was not just any radical vanguard project; as art historian Antigoni Memou summarizes, it was an effort at demolishing 'the status quo and all its structures'.[16] This included destroying capitalist consumer culture and stagnant state bureaucracies, but also ending the undemocratic treatment of women and people of color, as well as the vilification of the counterculture, which was by then influencing a new generation across several continents. The SI's avant-garde program prefigured much of the student movement's ideology, including its focus on autonomous organizational structure and youthful calls by protesters for *De omnibus dubitandum* (Latin for 'Everything must be doubted'). As Stevphen Shukaitis writes, the SI invoked 'a doubly articulated process of refusal: the refusal of separating art from daily life and the re-fusing of these antagonistic energies by capitalist production and governance'.[17] In the midst of upheaval, art was indeed fusing with life, and the SI's heady participation in May 1968 involved days and nights of blurred participation in political assemblies and committees, where 'workers and intellectuals from all over Europe, as well as many other parts of the world, [were] suddenly echoing such *internationaleries* ideas as, *all power to the imagination*,' observes the scholar Jelena Stojanovic. To this I would add such SI slogans as 'Take your desires for reality' and 'Beneath the paving stones – the beach.'[18]

But as much as the revolutionary moment was sudden and unpredictable, so too was its collapse. Not unlike the Commune of 1871 or the prior, year-long uprisings of 1848, the rebellions of 1968 came to an end abruptly. Armored tanks flanked the boulevards of Paris, as President Charles de Gaulle fled to neighboring Germany to garner additional military support, should France fall to the youthful insurrectionists. It did not. The country avoided a potential recapitulation of the Communards' tragic and bloody fate, though not without casualties. Across the globe, other assailed governments prevailed, often using far more repressive measures, as was the case in Mexico and Czechoslovakia. Precisely because of the widespread inclusiveness of the rebellion, its ultimate collapse was, especially for the SI, an epic historical setback, if not a disaster. Capitalism, however, would never be the same again.

SPLINTERS AND SHADOWS OF THE SI

After the revolution collapsed, the legacy of the SI – its theories, techniques and programs – drifted about, spoor-like, here and there, and yet, outside of a few small circles of artists and intellectuals in a handful of northern European cities, comprehensive knowledge about the movement remained sparse and uneven for decades. As the 1960s 'Great Refusal' morphed into the 1970s 'No Future' nihilism of the Sex Pistols, the SI's presence manifested most clearly in the worlds of underground cinema and punk music, as well as in such do-it-yourself (DIY) visual art forms as cheaply printed zines filled with cut-and-paste images and texts. It took another two decades before the SI practices of *détournement* and *dérive*, an uninhibited drift through urban spaces, reappeared; though in repurposed form as tactical media (TM), in which digital artists engaged in online hijackings, culture jamming (the disruption of mass media) and public interventions – topics that I explore in Chapter 7. Perhaps above all, it was the sequestering of Situationist theories within academia that delivered the real *coup de grâce* to the group's aspirations of countering the spectacle with the mass liberation of imagination. As Sven Lütticken comments, 'After May '68, the Situationist International found itself turned into "a collective star" by media and hangers-on', but it was a politically ineffective celebrity, whose revised postrevolutionary mission assured followers that 'the more famous our theses become, the more shadowy our own presence will be'.[19]

Like particles of non-reflective dark matter imagination, still unrecognized by the mainstream art world, the shadowy spirits of the SI have come to inhabit the unarticulated folds and fault lines of an otherwise coherent, or seemingly coherent, capitalist aesthetic apparatus. For many, if not most activists today, spaces of negation and rupture as Rancière insists, are the only possible counter-topographies imaginable wherein a radical politics might still thrive. Total subversion of the system and its spectacle is deemed impossible. Thus, it seems as if one half of the SI's project has survived – the negative, critical half of anti-spectacle – whereas their radical vision of an entirely different society, economy, architecture and urbanism springing from totally emancipated creativity has either been forgotten or dismissed as radical romanticism. But what if, nearly half a century onwards, the seeming triumph of capitalism's particular form of aesthetic totality, one that often appears as paradoxically fragmented, sets the very stage for a new iteration of the art of activism, and the activism of art?

For now, simply hold that thought. Discussed next is a different attempt at a 'Great Refusal', carried out by artists seeking to break free not only from the institutionalism of high culture but also a brutally oppressive military state. We remain in the consequential year of 1968 in order to investigate the consequences of a brief, but far-reaching encounter between an influential New York City art critic and a group of Argentinian artists struggling to transform their art into a direct activist weapon in the Global South.

Chapter 3

Grupo de Artistas de Vanguardia

> 'I said, "What kind of art are you making?" and they said, "We're not making art. We're not going to make art until the world is better."'[1]
> *Lucy R. Lippard*

Thanks to a fortuitous North-South encounter, the 1968 activist art project Tucumán Arde became known in the US precisely as artists in New York City and elsewhere were struggling to transform their work into a politicized tool that would be useful for the anti-war, anti-racist, pro-liberation mass movements of the late 1960s and 1970s. In September of that year, the New York City-based critic Lucy R. Lippard happened across *Grupo de Artistas de Vanguardia* while serving on a jury for an art prize in Buenos Aires. The loose-knit coalition of Argentinian artists was seeking to align its collective practice with workers, labor unions and leftist opponents of authoritarian President Juan Carlos Onganía's military dictatorship. Tucumán Arde, or 'Tucumán Is Burning', was the outcome: a multiphase, multimedia program and exhibition that called attention to the country's northeastern province of Tucumán, where a recently self-installed right-wing junta was carrying out harsh anti-labor policies and factory closings. Lippard discussed the project in her highly influential 1973 book *Six Years: The Dematerialization of the Art Object from 1966 to 1972*, and although her report was brief and inexact, the repute of Tucumán Arde has grown steadily since.[2]

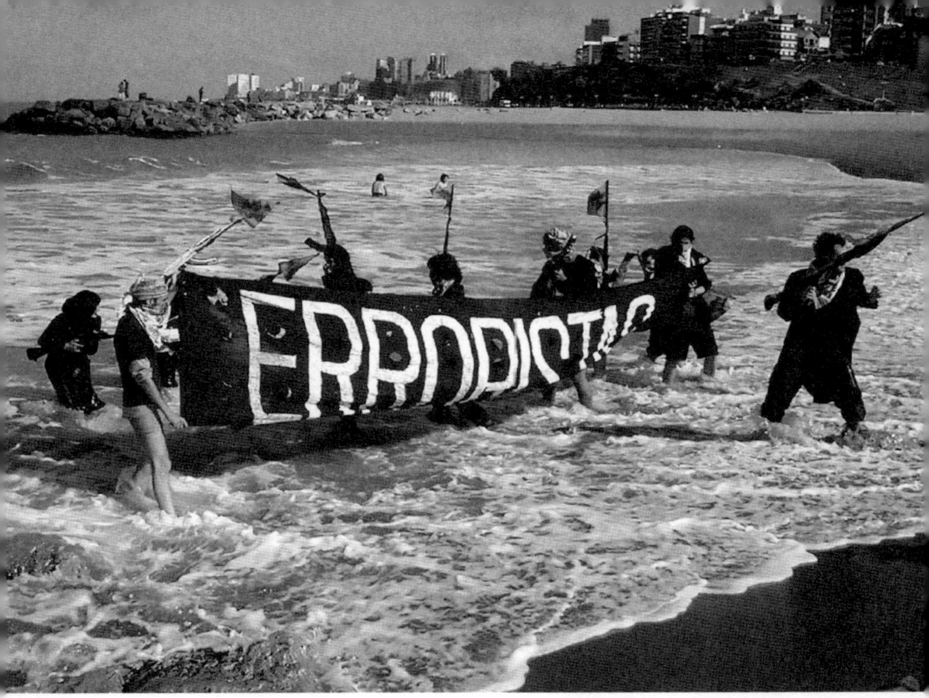

Fig.4 The Buenos Aires-based collective Etcétera stages a marine-style military invasion entitled International Errorista, carried out in 2005, directly below the flight-path of US President George Bush as he was arriving in the coastal resort city Mar del Plata for the Summit of the Americas.

Over the decades, and especially in recent years, the pivotal role of Grupo de Artistas de Vanguardia and their Tucumán Arde projects within any genealogical backstory of socially engaged art has been amplified by theorists, historians and researchers.[3] In 2010, Ana Longoni and Mariano Mestman published what is perhaps the definitive historical account, which informs this chapter.[4] Setting aside the issue of whether or not Tucumán Arde's now virtually legendary status introduces an alternative canon of socially committed art, I want to focus here on the group members' own conflict about their professional identity as artists, a debate that is still very much with us, more than 50 years on.

ART FOR THE PEOPLE (?)

Whatever ambivalence the SI expressed towards art, including rejecting its elitist history and privileged institutions, they nevertheless built upon and sought to exceed a long-standing avant-garde set of theories and practices that laid the groundwork for their critique of the mass spectacle. This paradox is summarized by Mikkel Bolt Rasmussen, who writes:

> With Dada and Surrealism it became obvious that the only true art was anti-art, that the authentic artwork carried its own negation. Dada and Surrealism had each driven art beyond its limits and carried out the self-transcendence of art ... they [the SI] made it clear that the time had now come to transgress Dada and Surrealism.[5]

But Grupo de Artistas de Vanguardia confronted a more immediately brutal adversary than that found in Paris in 1968 (though not in Algeria, whose revolution the SI supported), and did so from within a more orthodox, modernist-oriented art establishment than that of postwar Europe. While some group members in Argentina sought to repurpose their formal, academic training into a politically useful practice, others had never studied art – yet together, they generated a rich variety of artistic models and methods for visualizing dissent. Lippard observed at the time that they were also questioning such mainstream artistic attributes as 'permanence, commercialism, materialism, and chauvinism'.[6] Or, as Longoni explains, 'the Itinerary of '68 signaled a radical avant-garde confrontation with the artistic milieu, carried out through politically charged and explosive events that led to a final break with the art world.'[7]

Significantly, this break did not lead to a poverty of aesthetic means; instead, in order to convey the complexity of oppressive conditions under which Grupo de Artistas de Vanguardia worked, they employed a plurality of media and visual forms that ranged from photojournalism, street posters and graffiti to performative actions, interviews with striking workers and self-published research gathered on visits to the hard-hit region. Tucumán Arde also involved several phases of direct activist intervention that unfolded in the cities of Rosario, Buenos Aires and Santa Fe. Some of these events were produced in collaboration with the CGT (Confederación General del Trabajo) union, a broad, left-leaning political coalition conjoined by shared opposition to the dictatorship. And rather than display Tucumán Arde in a museum or art gallery, the group exhibited their work in spaces operated by the CGT union. On opening day, in a gesture prefiguring much socially engaged art today – but with a distinctly bitter twist – cups of sugarless coffee were served to visitors 'as an allusion to the sugar shortage brought about by refinery owners hoarding the sugar', Ana Longoni writes. Every few minutes, 'a blackout threw the building into darkness as a reminder that a Tucumán child was dying at these intervals'.[8]

Outwardly, the group's multiplicity of aesthetic styles and media tactics shares a resemblance to the Situationists' variegated production of manifestos, slogans, pamphlets and actions, including performative drifts in urban spaces and ironic hijacking of advertisements and state propaganda. Yet the SI appears to have had little direct influence on Grupo de Artistas de Vanguardia, even if a link is sometimes applied retroactively, in order to fit Tucumán Arde into a larger avant-garde historical narrative emanating from northern Europe. What is clear, however, is that while culturally divergent and physically separated by more than ten thousand kilometers, both the SI and Grupo de Artistas de Vanguardia sought to escape established art institutions, turning instead to forms of political activism that kept pace with the broader desire for sweeping, radical social changes.

For her part, Lippard was confounded, but also intrigued and ultimately politicized by her encounter with this group of Argentinian artists who were abandoning their professional status for political reasons. On her return to the US, Lippard saw the New York art scene with fresh eyes:

> They [the artists] were supposed to be the freest of all. Yet, in fact, the radicalization of a small sector of the art community led many artists to explore their own socially-conditioned prisons – to see how far esthetic freedom stretched, how much of it was illusory, and even how much their esthetics were determined by the institutions that decided their fates.[9]

In this sense, the aesthetic challenges faced by artists in the United States at the time were not entirely dissimilar from those of the creators of Tucumán Arde. With few historical or formal reference points to serve as a guide (a topic taken up in the next chapter), US artists, with mixed success, struggled to radicalize their practice in opposition to the war in Vietnam, among other political concerns. And there is another important historical detail also links the SI with Grupo de Artistas de Vanguardia, and to the burgeoning activist art then emerging in the US during the 1960s: a common effort to make art politically effective, and to utilize public spaces for its distribution, thus taking high culture away from elites and bringing it directly to the people. Of course, who exactly 'the people' consist of is a different and continuously morphing problem, as we shall encounter.

Even as US artists were poised to initiate a process of radicalization that was unlike anything witnessed since the Leftist art of the 1920s and 1930s, many members of Grupo de Artistas de Vanguardia had already abandoned their artistic practices. By the end of 1968, some, according to Longoni and Mestman, had moved directly into political activism, including armed struggle, and only decades later did a few finally return to art-making. As the historians bleakly report, the Tucumán Arde artists 'took a vow to never exhibit their works in art galleries or museums, never to submit them to salons, scholarships, prizes or any other institutional space ruled by bourgeois art'.[10] In short, Grupo de Artistas de Vanguardia sought to avoid all petty-bourgeois distractions and pretensions through a total rupture with high art institutions, followed by a descent into everyday movement activism.

It was unquestionably a severe decision, but one undoubtedly spurred by intensifying authoritarian state repression of workers, peasants, artistic vanguards and the burgeoning, youth-centered counterculture as a succession of dictatorial military juntas would come to rule over Argentina until 1983. Reflecting on this act of disengagement, Longoni later reflected that the artists of Tucumán Arde 'believed that the "new aesthetics" could preserve its revolutionary nature only if it kept away from the institutions of art', adding that in our time over 35 years later, 'the difference between the inside and the outside of these institutions seems rather blurred, and the boundaries are undergoing constant revision and re-formulation'.[11] Yet, like their counterparts in the US, artists trained in modernist forms who then search for a means of politicizing their practice often find themselves in limbo, floating somewhere between a schematic conception of 'the people' – or the 'working classes' or 'oppressed minorities' – and their own professional station in a society that allegedly expects them to remain apolitical, or merely token radicals, but always unconditionally 'free'. It may also be possible to explain this drastic withdrawal as a candid confrontation with what theorist Gene Ray describes as art's affirmative social function in a market-based economy, creating a situation that simply 'can't be reconciled within capitalism'.[12] For if, as the SI insisted, true artistic vanguardism died with Surrealism in the 1940s, then perhaps what replaced it following the defeated 1968 social uprisings was the unvanquished spectacle of capitalist consumerism hoovering up all the adventurous, youthful, experimental, nonconformist energy that remained, and of course without a political goal to reach towards other than self-satisfaction. But if so, how then to account for the surprising expansion of protest culture amongst professionally trained artists, throughout the 1960s and 1970s? It was a trend amongst small groups of highly politicized practitioners, intent on challenging the ideology of major cultural institutions, as well as a far larger, but less ideologically oriented multitude who joined mass organizations in which artists of all stripes demonstrated against war, fascism, militarism and especially nuclear weapons.

In the next two chapters I remain focused in and around the 1960s, in order to explore these forms of protest art mobilization, but also to examine a third manifestation of cultural activism, involving those artists who either turn their backs on the art world and embed themselves directly within social movements – as with some of the members of Tucumán Arde – or those organic 'movement artists' who develop, often autodidactically, from within the ranks of social organizations themselves. One important aim here is to spotlight the typically unacknowledged link between all these seemingly disconnected modes of protest aesthetics, as well as to challenge the allegedly ineffable boundary separating social movement culture from high art. Indeed, towards the conclusion of the book, we will witness the remarkable breaking down of these barriers in the 21st century, while asking why this is taking place today, and what this collapse might mean for both art and activism. In the history that immediately follows, clues to answering these questions are at least partially detectable.

Escaping the Long Greenbergian Shadow

> 'It just happens to be a noticeable fact that you have to have dignified leisure in order to cultivate taste in any of the arts, not the leisure of an unemployed stevedore.'[1]
> *Clement Greenberg*

> 'The AWC [Art Workers' Coalition] did not begin as a political group, but its models were clearly the Black and student movements of the 1960s.'[2]
> *Lucy R. Lippard*

Although not without pushback, it would be difficult to underestimate the degree of art world power wielded by the formalist critics, especially Clement Greenberg, over postwar Anglo-American artists and beyond. A relentless, often domineering advocate for modernist abstraction, Greenberg is best known for the 1939 essay 'Avant-Garde and Kitsch', which equated politically motivated social realism with sentimental populist propaganda. Likewise, his widely read 1960 essay 'Modernist Painting' claimed that realistic, naturalistic art had 'dissembled the medium, using art to conceal art'.[3] It is not surprising, therefore, to find one of the critic's foremost disciples, longtime *New York Times* art critic Hilton Kramer, denouncing a rare 1988 exhibition of political graphics at the Museum of Modern Art (MoMA) as echoing 'the bad taste of the 1920s' – a reference to the anti-capitalist imagery of William Gropper, Hugo Gellert and the leftist photographers of John Reed Clubs, whose work

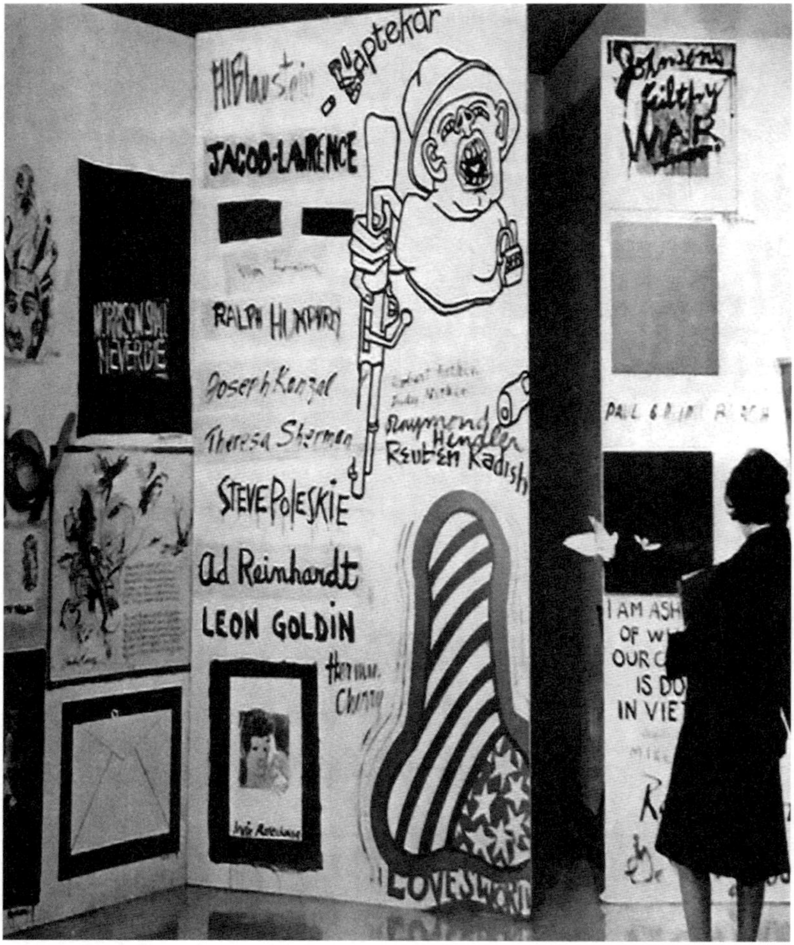

Fig.5 *Collage of Indignation* organized by Artists and Writers Protest at the Loeb Student Center, New York University, 29 January to 4 February 1967.

appeared in the pages of *New Masses*, a publication with ties to the Communist Party USA (CPUSA).[4] The 1988 exhibition was entitled *Committed to Print* and included radical ephemera and social movement art borrowed from the PAD/D archive, a collection that was later donated to the museum (discussed in Chapter 6). It's noteworthy to add that MoMA has never since attempted anything remotely resembling this exhibition of leftist graphics. Also worthy of mention is the seven years (1981–8) that PAD/D published a newsletter in which the group struggled to account for social movement culture as part of an expanded concept of contemporary art, acknowledging in the process a plethora of creative activity (dark matter) just outside the art world's horizon of visibility. (A link to online copies of these journals is found in the Archive section, p.169.)

OUT FROM THE POSTWAR SHADOWS

Decades after the appearance of 'Avant-Garde and Kitsch', artists seeking to address social or political issues still struggled with such anti-realism, anti-figurative bias. Independence from formalism could also be a lonely affair, especially if one was based in New York or London, Toronto or Sydney, and endeavoring to produce what Greenberg and the philosopher Theodor W. Adorno both labeled 'advanced art', work that was innovative, challenging and original.[5] The experience of the British conceptualist John Latham offers anecdotal evidence of the situation. After partially destroying Greenberg's book *Art and Culture* by biting into it and chewing several pages, Latham lost his part-time teaching post at St Martin's in London, in 1967. Needless to add, the residue of this bookworm-ish protest action, *Spit and Chew: Art and Culture*, is now in the collection of MoMA.

At the same time, any backstory for socially engaged art in the 1940s and 1950s must also take into account the US government's systemic destruction of leftist unions and political parties, a campaign that left many artists struggling more with expressing their inner demons rather than the external monsters of war, poverty, authoritarianism and racial injustice. Still, it was not an entirely apolitical interval. As the late art historian John Hutton pointed out, 'it is important to remember that the issue is not politicization per se, but the relative degree of political activity and political content in the work and lives of the artists and critics from the 1940s on'.[6] Artists may not have organized into Left-leaning protest coalitions as they did in the 1920s and 1930s, especially during the time of the anti-fascist Popular Front and American Artists' Congress, or as they would again during and after the tumultuous 1960s, but even such abstract painters as Robert Motherwell, Elaine de Kooning, Stuart Davis, Philip Guston and Barnett Newman spoke out against fascism in Spain and racism at home.[7] However, while they embraced a personal political stance in keeping with their leftist counterparts in Europe such as Pablo Picasso, Fernand Léger and René Magritte, or the painters and muralists Frida Kahlo, Diego Rivera and David Alfaro Siqueiros in Mexico, explicit politics was typically absent from their art – Philip Guston's early, 1940s pre-abstract works and Motherwell's *Elegies to the Spanish Republic* (1948–67) being two impportant exceptions. Still, the policed separation between politics and artistic practice only truly begins to erode in the next decade, fully collapsing in the 1970s as described in Chapter 5.

1960S USA

By the middle of the 1960s, growing support for the civil rights movement and feminism, as well as opposition to the Vietnam War, began to influence the social activity, if not always the visual practice, of many more artists. Feminists in particular raised issues with the artistic canon, mostly male but also mostly white, paving the way for an opening up of what, how and by whom art is produced. Meanwhile, some otherwise non-political artists participated as protestors, including the minimalists Donald Judd and Robert Morris for example, with no alteration to their abstract studio art practice at the time.

A smaller group with existing reputations leveraged their imagery in support of given causes, often in the form of posters or prints, such as Jasper Johns' signature *Flag* image, reproduced in 1969 as a lithograph and later reprinted with 'Moratorium' stenciled beneath to commemorate mass anti-Vietnam War resistance that same year. Or, a bit later, Andy Warhol's poster for the ultimately failed campaign of anti-Nixon presidential peace candidate George McGovern in 1972. Less known then, but gaining visibility today, were Black photographers such as LeRoy W. Henderson Jr and Roy DeCarava who, among other topics, documented civil rights protest activity and making such images of resistance integral to the broader social movement.

Crucially, from the mid-1960s onwards, a continuous and widening stream of mostly short-lived protest coalitions arose amongst artists, converging, disbanding and re-forming again, with a variety of shifting yet overlapping political agendas. This big bang expansion of socially engaged art permitted both established and emerging practitioners to add their cultural weight to anti-war, feminist, civil rights and other timely causes. One did not have to explicitly identify as a dissident to temporarily join a protest group. And unlike the activism of the 1920s and 1930s, participation was not being marshalled by a specific organization such as the Communist Party USA, or left-leaning unions. It was as though the cultural sector had become suddenly aware that it wielded a substantial political force all its own. American artists, including musicians, poets and novelists, were becoming more like European public intellectuals to whom the mainstream media turned for seemingly penetrating social insights. Even the US State Department briefly advocated for high culture including abstract painting because it allegedly signaled the extent of individual freedom possible under Western capitalism. With art museum attendance doubling between 1952 and 1962, and public fascination with Pop art leading the way, the visual arts were also becoming ever further integrated into what the Situationists labeled the 'spectacular industries', though not without hesitation and critical pushback.[8]

FROM ANGRY ARTS TO GUERRILLA ART ACTION GROUP

Despite the prevailing abstinence of explicit political content in the work of US postwar visual artists, a small number of painters with historical ties to earlier Left movements formed a contrary tendency, including the figurative artists Nancy Spero, Leon Golub and May Stevens, as well as Rudolf Baranik who described his approach as 'socialist formalism', a unique and eccentric amalgamation of politically charged content and Greenbergian abstraction.[9] Along with painter Alice Neel and Black artists such as Faith Ringgold, Benny Andrews and the far more senior painters Romare Bearden and Jacob Lawrence, not only was an ideological critique explicit in the work of certain dissident artists, but through alliances with writers, musicians and other artists they led collective opposition to US Cold War policies, including military intervention against the North Vietnamese. One prominent outgrowth of this cultural organizing was the 1966–7 project *Artists and Writers Protest.*

On 27 June 1966, the group ran a full-page *New York Times* statement that read, 'End Your Silence' over US involvement in Vietnam, signed by Golub, Spero, Stevens and Baranik, as well as abstract painters Lee Krasner and Mark Rothko, Fluxus artist George Brecht, minimalist Donald Judd, art historian Dore Ashton and such leading cultural figures as Hannah Arendt and Susan Sontag, among others. The group produced a portfolio of prints the next year with works by abstractionists Ad Reinhardt, Louise Nevelson and Mark di Suvero. Still more ambitious was the 1966 Peace Tower, aka *The Artists' Tower of Protest* on the West Coast, a 58-foot-tall steel structure designed by Mel Edwards and Di Suvero, both sculptors, with over 400 attached 2 × 2-foot individual painted panels. Still, the vocabulary of activist art was nascent at best and the panels primarily depicted geometric shapes or graphic designs, rather than anti-war statements. When an artist did include something politically explicit, it often consisted of a graphicly rendered slogan such as 'Peace' or 'Stop War in Vietnam Now'.

Back in New York City, another large-scale and collectively produced anti-war endeavor took place the following year. Angry Arts Week was a 1967 anti-war event that included a 36-meter-long *Collage of Indignation*, created by 150 artists (fig.5). During its exhibition run, hundreds of dancers, musicians, filmmakers and poets joined the event, and even compared the US involvement in Southeast Asia to the disastrous French colonial war in Algeria.[10] The recently formed anarchist art group Black Mask participated too, shortly before it went underground using the new moniker 'Up Against the Wall Motherfucker', a phrase taken from the poem 'Black People!' by LeRoi Jones, aka Amiri Baraka. And although Black Mask founder Ben Morea's abstract paintings were 'clearly executed under the influence of the second generation of Abstract Expressionist painters', as Nadja Millner-Larsen points out, Morea was also one of the very few US artists who closely followed the revolutionary theories of the European Situationists, only to be denounced by Guy Debord later that same year.[11]

In 1969, the reform-oriented cultural group Art Workers' Coalition (AWC) managed to convince the Museum of Modern Art (MoMA), Whitney and Jewish Museums in New York, along with a number of commercial art galleries, to close for one day in opposition to the Vietnam War. Earlier that year, AWC had submitted a list of '13 Demands' to the New York art world that included placing a section of MoMA under the direction of Black artists, paying rental fees to artists for displaying their work, and staying open 'on two evenings until midnight and admission should be free at all times' to accommodate the schedules of working-class people.[12] Only the idea of making museums more accessible to non-elites met with any success, via the establishment of a free night in early 1970. Lamentably, in recent decades, the free night has been rebranded by private corporate donors, thereby erasing and privatizing the gesture's historically activist roots in one fell swoop.

Also in 1969, Women Artists in Revolution (WAR), a feminist faction of AWC, and Women Students and Artists for Black Art Liberation, called for the inclusion of more women artists at MoMA and the Whitney Museum; while another group, the Black Emergency Cultural Coalition, targeted the exhibition *Harlem on My Mind: Cultural Capital of Black America, 1900–1968*, a Metropolitan Museum of Art project that consisted of enlarged floor to ceiling photographic images of African Americans, going about everyday activities in the uptown Manhattan neighborhood, yet contained no paintings or sculpture by Black artists, either dead or alive. The following year, 1970, witnessed a nationwide student walkout protesting President Nixon's expansion of military activity into Cambodia and the shooting and killing of student protestors at Kent State University in Ohio and Jackson State College in Mississippi. Members of Guerrilla Art Action Group (GAAG) staged a mock gun battle in front of the Museum of Modern Art, and a few weeks later hundreds of people participated in the New York Artists' Strike against Racism, Sexism, Repression and War, picketing the Metropolitan Museum after its board members refused to meet their demands to temporarily close as a protest against the Vietnam War.[13] The strike – which was among the first of its kind, though not the last – received endorsements from the Art Students' Coalition, Art Workers' Coalition, Women Artists in Revolution, United Black and Puerto Rican Artists, and Artists and Writers Protest.[14]

ARTISTS AS SOCIAL CRITICS

Protest by artists was therefore not necessarily the same as protest art, and most of these informally organized cultural associations faded within a year or two of their founding, but when considered together, and in relation to the SI in Europe and Tucumán Arde in Latin America, we can begin to gauge the precipitous outgrowth of art activism that emerged in the 1960s as an expansion that, despite transformations and patches of relative stagnancy, continues to this day. Which is to say, the emergence of the contemporary art of activism, and the activism of art so prominent in the early 21st century made its first appearance in the 1960s, though not as a cultural movement tied to a particular ideological outlook, but as *artist qua artist*, like the collectivized actions of a vocational association or social block convinced of its nonaligned political agency, and perhaps also of its uniquely prescient historical vision.

In any case, the 1960s marks the emergence of a dissident cultural paradigm within contemporary art, one that establishes a new horizon of possibilities sanctioning artists of many types, including modernist abstractionists, figurative painters, minimalists and those only moderately political in outlook, to engage in organized forms of protest as members of a seemingly independent artistic profession. And conceivably, it was the very legacy of 19th-century artistic autonomy and early-20th-century vanguardism that may have laid the groundwork for such faith in the exemplary social judgement and nearly oracular status of artists. Still, it is important to note that politically committed art-making also thrived *outside* the gates of the art world, within the organized agency of social movements, where no such claims of artistic autonomy or cutting-edge aesthetics are advanced, as shown in the next chapter.

Chapter 5

1968 and After: The Phantom Archive of Social-Movement Culture

> 'Things are made clear, almost like a language, and so art is a powerful tool to communicate with the community.'[1]
> *Emory Douglas*

Social movements generate copious amounts of ephemeral visual culture, from graphics in the form of flyers, pamphlets, graffiti, stencils, banners and posters, to performative events, pageants and experiences which amplify a particular movement's message, along with legislative activism and mass-media-oriented actions such as public protests, choreographed 'fake' die-ins (staged death by a nuclear weapon's blast for example), boycotts and mass arrests. Such protest aesthetics developed alongside postwar grassroots campaigns for Black civil rights, gay rights and women's liberation, as well as the anti-nuclear-power movement, and these varied cultural forms are continuously rediscovered and recycled, as if being drawn from some unseen archive brimming with protest aesthetic options. Consider the home-spun flags, shields and helmets produced by the Japanese Sanrizuka farmers who have, since 1966, collectively resisted first the construction and then the extension of Tokyo Narita Airport; or the didactic broadsides diagramming relationships between men's wage labor and women's unwaged housework by 1970s Lotta Feminista activists in Italy; or the satirical woodcuts made during the Gwangju Uprising in 1980s South Korea. Consider the 'Köpi [squatted

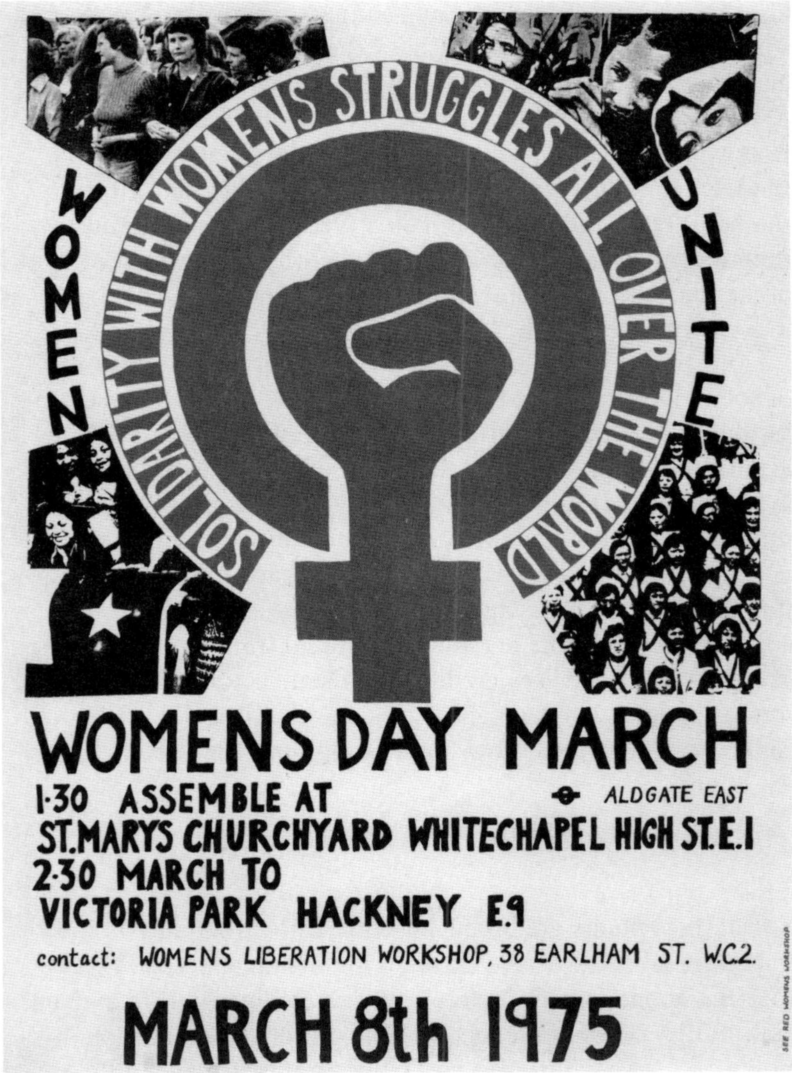

Fig.6 See Red Women's Workshop, *Womens Day March* poster, 1975, offset lithographic print, 42 × 30.5 cm.

housing project] Is Not for Sale' banners created by Autonomen squatters in 1990s West Berlin; or the street photography and guerilla theater of the South African collective Medu Art Ensemble operating in exile between 1977 and 1994 from Botswana; or the improvised street barriers generated by the UK's long history of anti-road protests that peaked in the late 1990s; and the *gilets jaunes* (yellow vests) anti-fuel tax movement in France (from 2018) with their repurposing of standard motorist emergency jackets (and not all social movements are strictly 'leftist').

One reason that the abundant visual and material culture of social movements is seldom exhibited in major art institutions is the tendency to disregard the lofty category of 'fine art' itself. Reciprocally, the dismissal of such grassroots protest art by mainstream institutions only guarantees that social movement culture's fidelity to genuine political transformation is deep, urgent and uncompromised. Perhaps most significantly, it is the multitudinous agency of social movements that has come to represent the default for political transformation today, at a time when the very credibility of state actors, parties and unions appears irredeemably tainted and politically ineffectual, reflecting a sentiment now dominating both the Left and the Right.

EXPEDIENCIES

Social movements are broad-based coalitions relying on mostly volunteer laborers whose extra-parliamentary methods seek to bring about specific, often localized changes within a given community of mutual concern. They differ from traditionally organized political parties and labor unions whose highly organized policies and platforms pivot on fidelity to a particular ideology and/or professional identity. And although parties and unions frequently cooperate with social movements, at times even taking on a leadership role (whether welcome or not), social movements appear almost spontaneous in origin, behaving like 'singularities that act in common', to cite the philosophers Antonio Negri and Michael Hardt, who prefer the term 'multitude' as a label for mass forms of agency that in more recent decades they envision as 'a fundamentally new kind of body, a common body, a democratic body', and in which 'new figures of struggle and new subjectivities are produced in the conjecture of events'.[2] Regardless of terminology, it is the stateless, de-territorialized power of this multitude that has come to define, for better and sometimes for worse, the broader politics of the Left in recent decades, far more so than the dominant ideologies, parties, unions and working class movements of the 19th and 20th centuries.

Likewise, social-movement culture and imagery is most often created collectively, sometimes by non-professionals and self-taught artisans, and the results typically go without attributed authorship – a significant missing detail that later hampers accurate research and preservation. These characteristics are precisely the opposite of the fine art tradition or that of the great auteur or genius. What's more, such work is easily marginalized because of its expediency. When a mass-movement campaign succeeds or fails, its imagery fades from sight and mind. If a few specimens are preserved, they often come to stand in for the whole: think of Lorraine Schneider's 1967 anti-war graphic whose renowned slogan 'War is not healthy for children and other living things' wraps itself around a colorful sunflower; or the Art Workers' Coalition's grisly 1969 protest poster, *Q. And babies? A. Yes, and babies*, in which a documentary photograph showing civilians murdered by US soldiers in Mỹ Lai Vietnam was held aloft before Picasso's *Guernica* when it still resided in the Museum of Modern Art (MoMA). Thus, despite representing considerable labor and historical value, the visual and material production of social movements is habitually treated as expendable, even by the members of the movements themselves, with the vast majority of social-movement artworks ultimately trashed, recycled or left in the streets where they disintegrate or are covered by new layers of posters, graffiti and commercial announcements. When specimens are found tacked to a bulletin board in a cafe, community center or church basement, say, or discovered folded up in a shoe box or stuffed inside a closet, such 'storage conditions' represent a conservator's worst nightmare.

But social-movement culture has also accomplished things that more enduring works of art created for galleries and museums only dream about. To cite just one example, after decades of authoritarian governance, Portugal overthrew its dictatorship in 1974, after which a cultural phenomenon emerged whereby, as art historian Cristina Pratas Cruzeiro explains, 'new terms entered the art lexicon, such as popular participation, collaboration, public space or urban space and the participation of non-artists in socially engaged artistic practices'.[3]

For movement artists and activists Josh MacPhee and the late Dara Greenwald, co-founders of Brooklyn's Interference Archive, social-movement culture introduces to art a type of aesthetic subjectivity whereby:

> people who previously did not consider themselves media or art producers emerge from struggles as artists, designers, and video makers – as well as organizers, communications specialists, publics speakers [thus establishing] more flexible definitions of who is or can be an artist.[4]

This is to say that social-movement culture redistributes technical and organizational expertise horizontally, amongst both trained and non-art participants, thus generating an unrestrained, DIY educational methodology in the service of something larger, more radical and hypothetically more revolutionary than merely the 'art world'. Why then has this complex realm of cultural production, with its claims about sweeping social transformation that resemble those of the historic avant-garde, remained almost entirely marginalized from the high art sphere of museums, academies and other art institutions? Counterintuitively, I will argue that movement culture has always intersected with, and at times significantly influenced, other artistic practices, including within the mainstream art world. Nevertheless, this cross-over effect has never been so evident as in recent years, not only because of the declining sovereignty of formalism and art-for-art's-sake, or the digitally networked visibility of previously excluded forms of artistic labor, but primarily thanks to the profound critical interrogation taking place over matters of historical appropriation and colonization, a process which is unsettling high culture's institutional authority from both within and below.

ART FOR AND BY THE PEOPLE?

Horizontal skill-sharing can be seen at work in the UK collective See Red Women's Workshop (1974–90), which began with three art students instructing other activists in the production of agitational and educational prints, T-shirts, posters and political cartoons in support of women's rights and socialism (fig.6). A similar process of self-education within a collectivized context took place in Los Angeles with the Peace Press, which operated between 1967 and 1987, and generated thousands of posters, pamphlets, flyers, newsletters and books for 'every progressive cause', including the American Indian Movement and United Farm Workers.[5] Likewise, the Chicago Women's Graphics Collective and New York City's ultra-Left Madame Binh Graphics Collective (MBGC), two all-women silk-screening groups, generated posters focused on feminism and Black liberation respectively. If any stylistic school or influence could be cited as common to these peripheral social-movement art practices, it would likely be the vivid graphic design style then coming out of post-revolutionary Cuba, a vibrant mix of anti-capitalist and Pop art-infused imagery that spread far and fast, influencing both professional and self-taught artists in Angola, Laos, Chile and in Southern California, where the Chicanx movement was then flourishing.

MBGC was a self-described revolutionary cadre, the Leninist-era term for a revolutionary group of intellectuals, who adopted their group name after Nguyễn Thị Bình, the only female signatory of the 1973 Paris Peace Accords in which the US withdrew from Vietnam. Like other social-movement groups discussed here, MBGC consisted of both art school trained participants and earnest social activists who combined labor and skills, not to produce art for the marketplace, but instead to support the May 19th Communist Organization, a faction of the former radical left-wing militant organization Weather Underground. In turn, May 19th and MBGC stood in solidarity with the Black Liberation Army (BLA). In 1979, when BLA member Assata Shakur escaped a New Jersey prison before re-emerging in Cuba later, the group produced a poster to be displayed in Harlem apartment windows: 'Assata Shakur is Welcome Here'. Still, as cadre member Mary Patten recognized decades later, the group operated on 'the margin of the margins, the periphery of the periphery'. Patten also situates the collective within a broader upsurge of activism in New York's art world at the time, pointing out that while it had been 'relatively quiet since the ferment of the U.S.-Vietnam war', after which, in the mid-1970s, there emerged a new wave of art activism from organizations such as '*Artists Meeting for Cultural Change*, the *Anti-imperialist Cultural Union*, *Art Workers' Coalition*, and the *Black Emergency Cultural Coalition* [that] were all part of the landscape'.[6]

Within this topography, peripheral social-movement artists such as MBGC sensed an ideological affinity with more politically informed cultural practitioners inside the art world, while also envisioning genealogical links to past forms of activist art. 'We learned to make silk-screened posters, like students in revolt internationally,' MBGC's Patten observed, referencing the Atelier Populaire of 1968 Paris, while also invoking the historical influences that her collective sought to incarnate.[7] Here was a true people's art, if not perhaps the authentic scion of the avant-garde tradition, seemingly free from the stain of co-optation and commodification – unlike, ironically, such radical formal practices as modernism, abstraction, Conceptualism and other 'failed' revolutionary cultural experiments now ensconced within museums, corporate lobbies and the homes of wealthy collectors.[8] Ironically, when such protest art and social-movement culture is noticed by the mainstream, it winds up out of site, in the museum's archival repository, as it is in MoMA for example with its PAD/D Archive mentioned in Chapter 4.

THE ARCHIVE AND ITS PHANTOM DOUBLE

On one level, the archive of social-movement art consists of whatever tangible documents, posters and so forth remain to be collected, categorized and studied. This is the obvious and manageable archive, accessible to scholars, though seldom featured in mainstream art exhibitions. At a different level though, there is the *other* archive, the shadowy one that is overflowing with a multitude of radical tropes which haunts our collective imagination. I will label this the 'phantom archive' of social-movement art. It is neither wholly material nor entirely abstract, instead existing in both registers simultaneously. Like an accumulation of artistic dark matter or a toolbox overflowing with visual motifs, it provides an invisible yet weighty mass of ideas, images and practices that typically go unseen – or may in fact be unseeable as proposed in Chapter 1 – from the perspective of the mainstream art world.

The phantom archive harbors both obvious and unexpected imagery: clichéd drawings of clenched fists in every possible style and medium, protesting crowds, movement flags, flowers and doves, but also renderings of people being tied and gagged or otherwise visibly repressed by police or military forces. There is also a repertoire of techniques and materials associated with this work, including banners, slogans hand-written in graffiti or rendered in oversize stencils, and, in a more recent context, the recycled pizza boxes, Amazon shipping containers and packing materials salvaged from dumpsters by protesters during Occupy Wall Street in 2011, for example. Indeed, cardboard has itself become a widely recognized signifier within contemporary art for the improvised urgent aesthetics of movement culture. This inventory of visual protest imagery serves up numerous default options for the artist who would be an activist, even as it torments orthodox art historical narratives that label it naive or kitsch. And indeed, from generation to generation, these archetypes reappear. Tellingly, even blue-chip artists turn to the imagery and techniques of social-movement culture when they feel called upon to make a political statement.

Consider a 1973 anti-war poster by Louise Bourgeois that repeats the word 'NO' in several types and sizes. The result does not much resemble her familiar, hand-drawn print style, but is more like a 19th-century anti-slavery broadside, as if the surrealist feminist artist had channeled centuries-old abolitionist 'message art' in a time-bending feat of automatic writing.

Likewise, Richard Serra's self-consciously artless, even childlike 2004 lithographic response to the disturbing photographs of hooded detainees being tortured by US officers in Abu Ghraib prison show the sculptor abandoning his signature geometric minimalist style to mimic the unschooled urgency of political graffiti. The artist scrawled 'STOP BUSH' beneath the image for an offset poster edition that protesters circulated widely at the Republican National Convention that year.

Yet even if social-movement culture's phantom archive has sporadically insinuated itself into the imaginations of contemporary artists, it was not until fairly recently that it was partially recognized by the mainstream art world. A primary reason for this is social-movement artists themselves who tended to shun establishment art institutions. Their reasoning is clear enough: the more activist imagery becomes disconnected from its active service to a particular social cause, the more it begins to appear as 'art', with all the class privileges associated with that term. From this perspective, the ephemeral posters, graphics and other time-sensitive imagery generated and ultimately left behind by activists, might be likened to cells shed by a collective body in constant motion, and the museum viewed as a dead zone inhospitable to activism. Meanwhile, from the institutional art world's perspective, such work is fundamentally utilitarian and therefore incapable of ascending to that particular Western ideal of non-functional aesthetic experience. Yet since the 1960s, the crossover between academically trained artists and social-movement artists has markedly increased, as social-movement culture's unwritten historical narrative and lineage of practitioners becomes ever more visible thanks to a new generation of activist artists and scholars, but also the spectacular ascendancy of the cyberspace.

Social-movement culture can therefore be likened to both a literal and figurative archive of images, ideas and techniques that hover, as if just off-stage, waiting to be accessed, repurposed and put to work. Today, access to this phantom archive is fundamentally enhanced by the distributive capacity of the Internet, cellular phones and digital technology in general, all contributing to a profusion of younger artists, many of color, dipping into this repository for inspiration (as well as on occasion the misappropriation of such imagery as happens when someone poaches from other people's cultural histories, without adequate insight or contextualization). And unlike in the past, this imagery now slowly finds its way into some mainstream art institutions, exhibitions, journals and collections. Take the case of American graphic artist Emory Douglas (b.1943) who emerged from the Black Power social movement of the 1960s, and more recently is being acknowledged as a fine artist in a more esteemed if customary manner.

Douglas initially studied industrial publishing technology while in juvenile detention, before focusing on graphic design at the City College of San Francisco. When in 1967 he became the minister of culture for the Black Panther Party, Douglas transformed the group's freely distributed newsletter into a showcase for revolutionary Black liberation imagery, not unlike the way John Heartfield reimagined the cover of the workers' weekly magazine *AIZ* as a vehicle for his anti-fascist photomontages in 1930s Germany. It took more than four decades after Douglas began his work with the Black Panthers for museum exhibitions to showcase his art in San Francisco, Los Angeles, New York, near Rotterdam in the Netherlands, all in 2019. In truth, activist artists like Douglas, who have embedded themselves in social-movement culture, seldom received even this degree of attention from mainstream art institutions and historians in the past. But especially following the street activism of 2020, work inspired by social-movement culture, including the imagery of Shellyne Rodriquez, Ramiro Gomez, Andrea Bowers and Narsiso Martinez, is receiving justified attention. Likewise, the superabundance of graphics and street art associated with Black Lives Matter now crosses over into visibility, if not hypervisibility. To wit, the phantom archive is far less ghostly and inaccessible than ever before, especially within the networks of cyberspace and increasingly in mainstream art venues. What comes next is the search by professionally trained, 1970s artists who struggled to find a new means of expressing political concerns directly within their studio practices. We also discover the first incendiary sparks challenging the dominion of European and Anglo-American art that is a pivotal feature of 21st-century activist art, and beyond.

1970s: The Activist Turn in Art

'Only through an exchange of ideas beyond the constraints of the institutional or academic space can we hope to see the light at the end of the bourgeois tunnel.'[1]
Rasheed Araeen

'What was new and significant about art in Britain during the 1970s was its repoliticization and feminization, its attempt to reconnect to society at large.'[2]
John A. Walker

'Official culture can only diminish our ability to understand the world and to act upon that understanding. The critical examination of culture is thus a necessary step in gaining control over the meaning we give our lives.'[3]
Artists Meeting for Cultural Change

For a time in the 1960s, Conceptualism appeared capable of tearing contemporary art away from its dependency on capitalism and the production of monetizable objects. Dry textual statements, invisible sculptures, didactic reading rooms and social game theory are some of the many 'dematerialized' forms that art began to take on at this time. Yet, as early as 1973, critic Lucy Lippard observed, 'hopes that "conceptual art" would be able to avoid the general commercialization, the destructively "progressive" approach of modernism, were for the most part unfounded.'[4] Such realizations may explain why

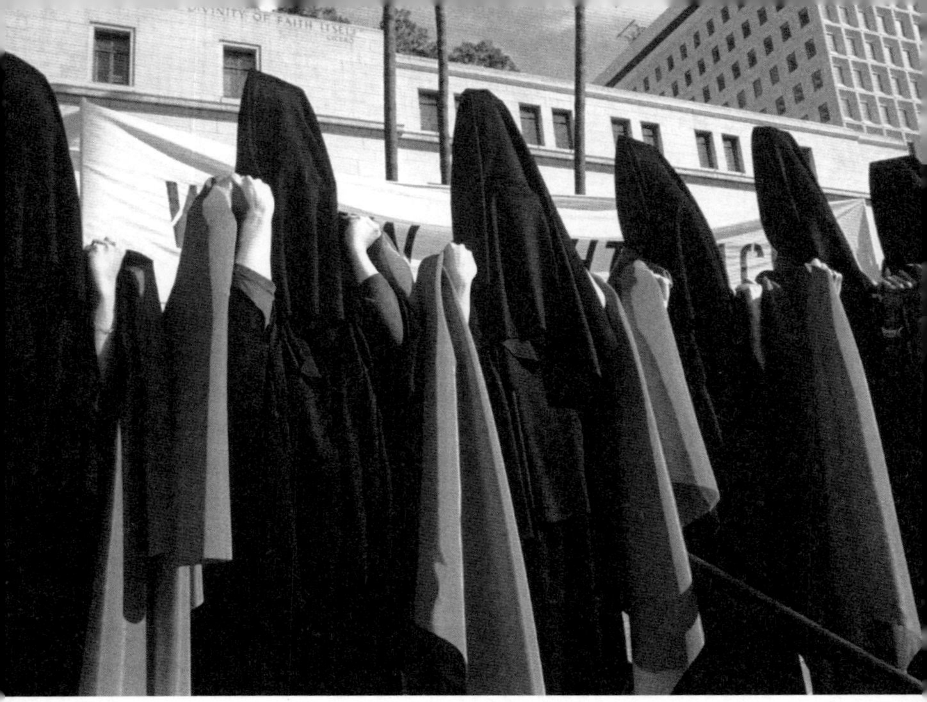

Fig.7 *In Mourning and in Rage*, a performative media intervention on the steps of Los Angeles City Hall, organized by Suzanne Lacy and Leslie Labowitz-Starus with participants from the L.A. Woman's Building, Rape Hotline Alliance and the City Council, December, 1977. Photo Maria Karras.

some 1970s politically aware artists abandoned 'advanced art' in search of a way to subvert the art world's process of 'commodifying dissent', as Thomas Frank later branded the capitalist spectacle's ever-expanding appropriation of nonconformist counterculture.[5] Others simply dropped out – as we witnessed with artists in 1968 Argentina – by joining social movement groups or trade unions where they worked as organizers and in-house graphic designers, as if submission to a radical cause was the surest way to avoid market cooptation while rejecting the privileged role of artistic auteur. In a sense, the very idea of becoming a 'cultural worker', a term frequently applied at the time, as opposed to an *artiste*, suggested that one's artistic labor was no more or less exceptional than that of a taxi driver, schoolteacher or industrial machinist. Of course, it is always more complicated.

ART WORKER, ART WORKER: WHAT WERE YOU THINKING?

Looking back, it is easy to see how the term art worker or cultural worker, with its likely origins in the 1930s and the American New Deal agency the Works Progress Administration, became charged after the 1960s with political entanglements, if not also misgivings that are more apparent today, decades later. For example, while the successful sculptor Carl Andre stated in 1976 that 'the position of the artist in our society is exactly that of an assembly line worker in Detroit', his remarks elicit unease if not exasperation now, especially considering the position of real workers ensnared within an alienating industrial factory. Indeed, a few years prior to Andre's comment, Kenneth Cockrel, co-founder of the League of Revolutionary Black Workers in Detroit, made his own compelling commentary about assembly-line work:

> They give you little bullshit amounts of money – wages and so forth – and then they steal all that shit back from you in terms of the way they have their other thing set up, that old

> credit-stick-'em-up gimmick society – consumer credit – buy shit, buy shit – on credit.[6]

But Andre's uncomfortable declaration also underscores two significant and contradictory trends of the time: first, a recognition that the rapid commercialization of even the most 'advanced' forms of art was reducing creative production to something resembling commodity manufacturing, especially if we think of the art world as a thin segment of the broader 'culture industry';[7] and second, a genuine desire by artists to demystify their elite status along with the type of work they carry out, both within and presumably for society. The contradiction reflects an ambivalence about artistic identity that is at once heartfelt and perplexing, one that had long been debated within avant-garde circles, including by the Situationists, and Grupo de Artistas de Vanguardia in Argentina, but also as far back as the Soviet vanguard in the early 20th century.

Efforts by professionally trained artists to find a way out of the conundrum of their simultaneously elevated and alienated social positioning, including attempts to 'exit' art altogether, run like a red thread, or a twisting steel conveyor belt, through the 1970s and later decades, up until today. It is an important theme of this book. And by the second half of the decade, with financially deteriorating conditions fueling capitalist opposition to the welfare state, thereby paving the ideological ground for the return of laissez-faire capitalism as neoliberalism, a series of templates had emerged, demonstrating ways that the contemporary artist might become a politicized activist, while still remaining an 'artist'. The new models did not only involve joining a protest group, as was common in the 1960s, but instead, creatively and intellectually laboring in collaboration with others to understand the social dilemmas inherent to art as a type of work. One New York City-based collective of primarily white, highly educated and politically minded artists, critics and art historians even attempted to consolidate the fragmented cultural resistance of the 1970s into something resembling a full-blown political art movement.

Artists Meeting for Cultural Change (AMCC) was formed in New York City in December 1975 in response to a specific event: the Whitney Museum's bicentennial exhibition *Three Centuries of American Art*, consisting exclusively of works from the collection of the nation's first billionaire, John D. Rockefeller III. Accusing the museum of class bias, sexism and racism, the group pointed out that of the 104 works in the exhibition, none was by a Black person and only one by a woman, an all too predictably and safe Impressionist painting by Mary Cassatt. After a letter-writing campaign and a picket line outside the Whitney Museum, AMCC produced 'an *anti*-catalog', a publication resembling John Berger's television series and later book *Ways of Seeing*, in which a series of collectively produced essays called the 'neutrality of art into question' – a statement the AMCC insisted was 'in reality, no more political than the viewpoint of official culture'.[8] They wrote:

> We [the editorial collective] share the belief that culture should no longer exist merely as an extension of the economic interests or the personal 'tastes' of the wealthy and powerful. Nor can we hope to transform culture outside of a struggle to transform the society from which it springs.[9]

The publication's multi-authored content foreshadowed the coming of social art history, an approach to cultural scholarship that today influences virtually all research in the field. Social art history is distinguished by the way in which it links art objects to a given social and political context (much as I am seeking to do in this volume, but with less focus on objects and more on actions and agencies). *An* anti-*catalog* featured essays entitled 'Black Art and Historical Omission', 'Looking for Women' and 'The Love of Art and the Art of Public Relations'. It also included critical reflections on Native American art and John D. Rockefeller's 1932 confrontation with Diego Rivera over the inclusion of Lenin in a mural commissioned for Rockefeller

Center (Lenin was ultimately removed). What makes *an anti-catalog* significant for any timeline delineating the rise of activist art is the project's innovative approach to cultural scholarship and the way it reflects the changing subjectivity of socially committed artists during the interlude between the defeated rebellions of 1968 and the triumph of neoliberalism.

POST-CONCEPTUAL POLITICAL PRACTICES

The debate about the artist as social agent took on different forms depending on the type of art one was already producing before political awakening. Some artists, particularly those linked with 1960s conceptual and performance art, continued to seek ways of reducing or eliminating object-making, often turning to dispassionate forms of photography, video and performance as a way to deprive the spectacle of commodified expressivity or pleasure. Between 1974 and 1975 Martha Rosler produced her now iconic video *Semiotics of the Kitchen* and the photo-conceptual piece *The Bowery in two inadequate descriptive systems*. The first addressed the patriarchal representation of women as nurturing, apron-wearing home workers; the second focused on photojournalism's perverse fascination with images of abject poverty and chemical addiction. Most importantly, Rosler approached the field of fine art as a consequential site for political intervention in itself, a lesson learned from her experiences as a woman artist, intense discussions taking place within feminist art circles, and groups such as AMCC, where the very question of whether high culture could be a medium of radical social change was hotly debated.

In 1971, the Guggenheim Museum canceled a solo exhibition by the artist Hans Haacke, a cofounder of the Art Workers' Coalition, ostensibly over a pair of data-driven visualizations tracing actual real estate holdings by New York City slumlords. The coolly conceptual projects were neither polemical nor accusatory, yet they were denounced by then Guggenheim Director Thomas Messer as an 'alien substance' that the 'art museum organism' must fend off.[10] Following this event,

Haacke's work moved away from its earlier focus on ecological and cybernetic systems toward exposing the hidden economic power of the art establishment and its corporate sponsors. By the early 1980s, Haacke had gone in a still more explicitly political direction, following the elections of conservative, anti-unionist UK Prime Minister Margaret Thatcher and US President Ronald Reagan. From conceptualist documentarian, to social critic, Haacke provided a canny, early analysis of the neoliberal agenda to do away with four and a half decades of state-sponsored social security programs.

The artist's new approach included two bitterly ironic oil portraits of the new leaders (1982 and 1983 respectively), as well as the incorporation of sly visual references aimed at demystifying the sanctity of both high political office and high art institutions. For example, Haacke's 1985 piece *MetroMobiltan* consisted of a large, faux, Beaux-Arts roof ornament modeled after New York's Metropolitan Museum of Art that hovers above a series of exhibition-style banners extolling Mobil oil corporation's financial support for African art on one hand, while acknowledging (in their own words) that they also supply essential petroleum reserves to the South African 'police and military forces', in defiance of a widely recognized boycott of the apartheid state. The crucial cultural link is the role that corporate largess plays in the art world by cushioning knowledge of institutionalized racism for museum audiences primarily made up of respectable political liberals.

Toronto-based artists Carole Condé and Karl Beveridge produced a graphic novel in 1975 based on similar Maoist publications entitled *It's Still Privileged Art*, its theme underscoring growing doubts about the ideology of high culture, while San Diego-based photo-conceptualist Fred Lonidier was actively exhibiting his work with labor unions instead of art galleries. Two years later, as though aiming to completely jettison this space of privilege, artists Suzanne Lacy and Leslie Labowitz-Starus orchestrated *In Mourning and In Rage*, an elaborate anti-femicide performance staged specifically for mass-media consumption on the public steps of Los Angeles

City Hall, as opposed to the limited audience who attend museums or art galleries (fig.7). Denouncing sensationalist news coverage of the 'Hillside Strangler' murders, their project opened up both a performative and tactical approach to leveraging the power of mass media through art that would influence groups such as Gran Fury, the Guerrilla Girls and RTMark/The Yes Men in the 1980s and 1990s.

This turn towards politicizing artistic practice was not limited to the United States. In the UK in 1974, the recently formed Artists' Union presented *United We Stand: Exhibition in Solidarity with the Miners*, not in an art gallery but, as though channeling Argentina's Tucumán Arde project, in the Trades Union Congress headquarters, Westminster, London. Subsequently, in East London in 1980, the feminist photographic poster collective Hackney Flashers amplified its ongoing street-art activism with an educational project created for schools and community groups; it contained a sheet of 35mm slides with a printed pamphlet entitled *Domestic Labour and Visual Representation*.[11] Like many other works cited in this book, the Flashers' project reflected a strong pedagogical commitment that has come up repeatedly among activist artists, especially from the 1970s onwards. This may be due to the increasing influence on artists of such academic fields as semiotics, feminism and critical theory, although as Lucy Lippard understood activist art in 1984, education was central to its practice: as she said, it must take place partially outside the art world to include some 'teaching and media practice as well as community and labor organizing [and] public political work'.[12] This facet of socially engaged art re-emerged more explicitly and concretely after the 1990s, to the point where it earned its own moniker: 'the Educational Turn in Art'.[13]

Also in London, the Pakistan-born artist Rasheed Araeen who started his career as one of Briton's leading 1960s minimalists, began to gather and compose newspaper clippings in the 1970s to expose the activity of the far-right National Front, as well as police repression of working-class and Black people in the UK. Later, Araeen founded the influential theoretical journal *Third Text*, an academic, peer-reviewed reincarnation of his previous, short-lived publication *Black Phoenix* (1978–9), in which the artist asserted that 'neo-colonialism is now being "brought" home to the metropolis of the capitalist world, for there exists a people within the Western world that must be neo-colonised and marginalized'.[14] Araeen's movement from minimalist to activist took place against the backdrop of several highly publicized, violent confrontations between British police and Black, poor, anti-fascist youth in 1977 in Lewisham, a borough of London, followed by a series of uprisings in the Brixton area, as well as Toxteth in Liverpool, Birmingham, Manchester and Leeds. The Black Audio Film Collective, a less explicitly ideological group seeking to reimagine documentary forms in terms of the Black British experience, emerged during the same period.

By the end of the 1970s, the tide had turned to the point where activist movements were giving clear political weight to cultural projects, as evidenced by the *International Art Exhibition in Solidarity with Palestine*, organized by the curator Rasha Salti and scholar Kristine Khouri in 1978 in Beirut, and by the Artists of the World against Apartheid, a widely exhibited archive of anti-racist artworks initiated by the French Fluxus artist Ernest Pignon-Ernest and Spanish writer and artist Antonio Saura two years later in 1980. Meanwhile, in Mexico, several activist collectives incorporated anti-US positions in their work, including Grupo Proceso Pentágono, Grupo Suma, Taller de Arte e Ideología and Tetraedro, all of whom were invited to participate in the 1977 Paris Biennale. Notably, some of these groups had emerged in the aftermath of the 1968 Tlatelolco student massacre carried out by the Mexican Armed Forces, equipped with weapons, ammunition and communications equipment that the US had provided for security during the concurrent Olympic Games. Grupo Proceso Pentágono was known for staging mock kidnappings and automobile accidents in Mexico City to protest against highways and housing projects that separated residents from communal gathering spaces. All four collectives ultimately agreed to collaborate on subverting the Paris Biennale by publishing their own independent counter-catalogue that included an essay by pro-Cuban novelist Gabriel García Márquez and denounced illegal, US-backed, anti-leftist terror campaigns such as Operation Condor, in which right-wing dictatorships began targeting dissident students and workers for assassination across South America, starting in 1975.[15] And in Chicago, the Chicago Surrealist Group, founded in 1966, became increasingly involved with Students For a Democratic Society (SDS) and with activists formerly affiliated with the Industrial Workers of the World (IWW or 'Wobblies'), publishing essays by Black Marxist intellectual C.L.R. James, proposing tantalizing links between anti-racist art movements in mid-20th-century America and the political and artistic avant-gardes at the turn of that century many decades earlier. Penelope Rosemont, who co-founded the Chicago Surrealists with her husband Franklin, wrote in 1978 that Surrealism is nothing less than 'an unrelenting revolt against a civilization that reduces all human aspirations to market values'.[16]

ARTISTS MEETING FOR CULTURAL CHANGE: TOO EARLY/TOO LATE?

Throughout the 1970s and continuing into the 1980s, artists who sought to contribute to the mass movements of their day, but were not interested in prolonged theoretical debates or transforming their practices into a directly political medium, continued to engage as provisional cultural activists. Consider this list of short-lived, movement-type groups and coalitions that existed between 1979 and 1982: Artists Against Nuclear Madness, Artists for Survival, Performers and Artists for Nuclear Disarmament, and Women's Pentagon Action, as well as the feminist groups No More Nice Girls, Heresies Collective, and Carnival Knowledge. In addition, exhibitions such as the *Anti-WW3 Internationalist Art Show* and *The Real Estate Show* protested against militarism and real estate speculators respectively. During this same period, longer-lived collectives also established themselves. Sisters of Survival (1982–6) in Los Angeles and in New York City, World War Three Illustrated (1979 to present), Paper Tiger Television (1981 to present), Group Material (1979–97) and Political Art Documentation/Distribution (PAD/D, 1980–7). It was a revival of cultural collectivism both similar to, and yet different from that of the 1960s, as will be discussed regarding the last two collectives in the following chapter.

Meanwhile, after seeking without success to formulate a cohesive or unifying position about art and social change, Artists Meeting for Cultural Change (AMCC) exhausted itself before the start of the 1980s. As former member and *anti-catalog* contributor Alan Wallach later reflected, AMCC's politics represented 'a characteristic mid-1970s muddle', a mix of 'anchorless liberalism, radicalism, and defeatism' in the aftermath of the civil rights movement, the dissolution of the New Left and the end of the War in Vietnam. Despite a year of feverish meetings in search of 'principles of unity', he added, the group failed to 'ignite a national protest movement in the arts'.[17]

And yet, beneath the ideological disorientation of the 1970s and the striving for a resolution to the art versus activism paradox, it is possible to see that AMCC's grand ambitions were delimited by the rise of cultural politics itself, a significant socio-political turning-point discussed in the next chapters. Moreover, like many artists and art projects at the time, AMCC was also dependent on state financial sponsorship that, minimal as it was, could only have complicated its revolutionary aspirations. By aiming to reprise that seemingly singular moment when being a socially engaged artist was, as Walter Benjamin had stipulated in 1934 with his influential anti-fascist text 'Author As Producer', a demand for partisanship in the good fight of class struggle, AMCC can be viewed as tragically ensnared in a transitional moment between the Left's critique of a failing liberal welfare state and its absence of preparation for the coming neoliberal, ultra-free market ideology that was just around the corner. In other words, AMCC's analysis arrived either too early or too late, just as perhaps the activist turn of the 1970s in general was destined to constitute a political paradox. Nevertheless, AMCC did achieve – by way of its weekly meetings, critical discourse and of course the *anti-catalog* – a direct and lasting influence on such emerging 1980s collectives as Group Material and PAD/D, to which I now turn: two activist organizations that simultaneously embodied the last radical remnants of 1968, while also paving the way for the enigmatic art of activism – and activism of art – that we witness today.

Chapter 7

1980s: Artists Respond to the Neoliberal Turn

'There is a key element in this 'new art' which has its counterpart in the business world. That element is innovation – without which it would be impossible for progress to be made in any segment of society.'[1]
John Murphy

'Art – or more broadly, "creativity" – has become the linchpin of the workfare system, in the financialized era of image and sign production.'[2]
Brian Holmes

'Although we didn't receive much credit in the mainstream, I think we and the other groups of the late 1970s were fuel for the political art boom of the late 1980s and early 1990s.'[3]
Jerry Kearns

The twin recessions of the 1970s followed years of economic downturn in New York City, and other former industrial centers, caused by a prolonged fiscal crisis from falling profits, spiraling oil prices and government disinvestment, but also exacerbated by white working-class taxpayers leaving cities for suburbia. Such 'white flight' was initiated in part by racial biases, but aided and abetted by what Guy Debord labeled 'the dictatorship of the automobile'.[4] In 1974, the rate of US economic growth as measured by GDP fell precipitously to negative 5 per cent, with similar contractions taking place in

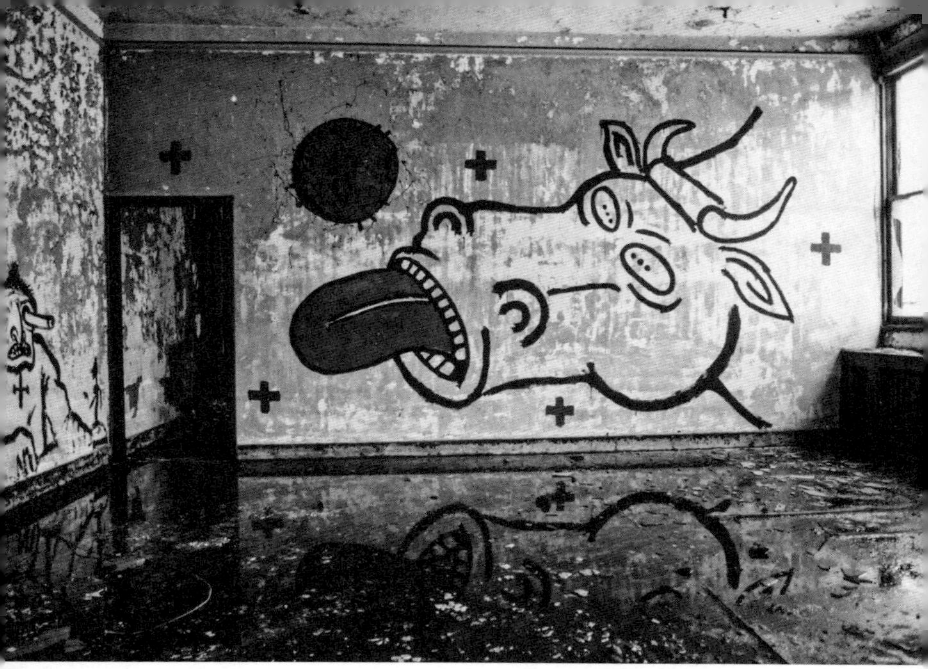

Fig.8 Gagging cow mural by David Wojnarowicz inside Pier 34 NYC, 1983, a crumbling waterfront shipping structure illicitly frequented by artists and gay men during the 1970s and 1980s, and demolished in 1984. Photo Andreas Sterzing.

the UK and Europe during the second half of the decade. This fiscal decline, combined with substantial job outsourcing to low-wage states and nations in the Global South, left many northern workers who remained in cities suffering from severe unemployment and rising homelessness. Communities of color were especially hit hard, with major metropolitan regions quite literally collapsing from defunded infrastructure, as banks and local municipalities refused to lend capital or redlined low-income neighborhoods with predominately non-white populations. All the while, austerity budgets were imposed on urban residents including givebacks from unionized workers and funding cuts to public schools, libraries, hospitals and transportation. And yet within this multipronged disaster site, artists working in community settings repurposed and reinvented the terms of survival itself.

CULTURAL POLITICS AND THE RISE OF NEOLIBERAL CAPITALISM

Before continuing, it is crucial to further unpack the significance of the 1980s as a key turning point in my narrative, not only for activist art or contemporary high culture, but for Western-style capitalist societies across the planet. Consequently, the tactical approach to both new media and public space as practiced with a remarkable degree of virtuosity by the AIDS-activist group Gran Fury and feminist art gang Guerrilla Girls in particular, also signaled that an intensified phase of spectacularization was evolving thanks to the virtually unopposed ascendency of global capital in its resurrected, laissez-faire incarnation, aka neoliberalism. The impact of these changes on art and culture, as argued here, include the overt adoption of methods associated with advertising, its graphics and distribution techniques, as opposed to street stencils and art carried aloft in public protests adopted from social-movement culture, with PAD/D being a primary example of the latter. Culture as the space in which to express dissent, but also identity, especially one repressed by the mainstream, was itself becoming a political force in its own right, aside from specific oppositional parties, unions, concepts such as class struggle and anti-imperialist emancipation, or even the ballot box. Still, this transformation was itself several decades in the making.

According to historian Michael Denning, immediately following World War II, triumphant Americans began to understand that culture was something the entire population had access to – which is to say that it was no longer just for wealthy elites, the State, or corporate media, but also a widespread social reality that was quickly gaining political strength and momentum. 'Suddenly, after 1950,' he writes, 'everyone discovered that culture had been mass-produced like Ford's cars; the masses had culture and culture had a mass.'[5] Growing capitalist markets generated an ever-expanding population of consumers in the North, while those struggling against colonialism and those in the socialist East were gradually lured into active participation within the marketplace, oftentimes through informal shadow economies. However, at the same time, Denning observes, cultural politics could also be measured by the rising youthful counterculture of the 1960s, along with a growing interest in the music, writings and art of the working class and people of color, whose media visibility and commercial viability were often enhanced, rather than hampered, by clumsy state efforts to suppress their influence.

Thus far, Denning's narrative keeps pace with that of the SI's Society of the Spectacle; except for the historian, it is the loss of mass party politics, a shift celebrated by the Situationists, that helps lay the groundwork for neoliberalism. Prior to this swerve towards cultural politics he argues, revolutionary organizing typically involved the building of a mass vanguard party, followed by the seizure of state power, either by parliamentary means or insurrection. As that possibility waned on the Left in the postwar era, due to a combination of US counterintelligence activity, the overt persecution of radicals in Hollywood and beyond, but also the 1956 exposure of Stalin's atrocities in the USSR, the very idea of the artistic avant-garde as the sharpest edge of a history-shaping vehicle also began to decline. What took the place of mass politics was an array of diverse oppositional positions and subjectivities. Visualize the myriad protest elements of the 1967 *Collage of Indignation* in Chapter 3, peeling away from their shared backgrounds and marching off in various directions, sometimes coordinated with other liberated images, at other times simply going in their own particular direction. What changed, in other words, with the defeated, or at least incapacitated revolutionary spirit of 1968, was the abandonment of the idea of revolution as an event, and the liberation of state power as its guarantee. Replacing this came a 'long march' of low-key resistance that, as Tony Negri, Paolo Virno and other Marxists of the Italian 'workerism' movement (*operaismo*) put it in their 1977 statement, 'Do You Remember Revolution?', would now have to thread its way 'through the workplaces, the organisation of social knowledge, the alternative economy, local services, administration and communications'.[6]

In the postwar period, that long march gradually moved into the spaces of everyday life, rather than the streets and squares and television stations of the system; it also inevitably modified the processes of production. In fact, as far back as 1963, SI member Alexander Trocchi published a manifesto that in retrospect seems to lay the groundwork for this inner turn towards cultural politics, by insisting that:

> the cultural revolt must seize the grids of expression and the powerhouses of the mind. Intelligence must become self-conscious, realise its own power, and, on a global scale, transcending functions that are no longer appropriate, dare to exercise it. History will not overthrow national governments; it will outflank them. The cultural revolt is the necessary underpinning, the passionate substructure of a new order of things.[7]

Unfortunately, post-1970s neoliberal capitalism has since selectively appropriated these same ambitions, just as it has the counterculture and the artistic avant-garde. So conspicuous is this takeover of 1960s Left radicalism and cultural vanguardism by the marketplace that in 1999 two French sociologists, Luc Boltanski and Eve Chiapello, described it as 'the new spirit of capitalism'.[8] Their analysis details how postwar, but especially post-1968, capitalist business theory actively incorporated antithetical forms of behavior into its modus operandi, including workplace dissent, imaginative flexibility and thinking outside the box, all of which were implemented at every level, from the manager down to the cubicle slave. The stage was therefore already set by the early 1970s for the rise of the reputed 21st-century 'knowledge worker' and 'creative class', decades before the arrival of the Internet made such a workforce realizable in practice. These conditions gave rise to new tensions and contradictions in the relationship between labor and capital, with a direct impact on the agency of political radicalism. As Hong Kong-based theorist Lee Chun-Fung summarizes these changes in relationship to cultural activism:

> in contrast to the traditional ideological forms such as class movements and decolonization movements, activism tends to refer to the movements that emphasize autonomy and spontaneity, and are usually not attached to a particular political party or ideological position based on ideology or party affiliation.[9]

1970S: PAYBACK AND AUSTERITY

In New York City, late-1970s austerity measures were aimed at paying back a massive bailout owed to a cabal of banks and creditors who floated the city's debt after it nearly went bankrupt in 1974. Indeed, the ultra-gentrified metropolis that we know today is essentially the outcome of this Faustian bargain, which traded off an affordable, diverse city for one dominated by relatively new, ultra-wealthy residents and the finance, insurance and real estate (FIRE) industries. Nevertheless, the severe economic crisis also led to the opening up of urban structures to squatters, alternative art spaces and community programs. Situated amid infrastructure dereliction and an excess of housing and commercial stock due to landlord neglect, these zones of social agency paradoxically gave rise to what Nandini Bagchee calls counter-institutions: insurgent, grassroots activism that provided 'direct deliverables and generated alternative forums of empowerment to communities under pressure'.[10]

The repurposing of a former public school on New York's Lower East Side by the CHARAS/El Bohio Community Center in 1979 is exemplary of these projects. Its mission reflected the Puerto Rican and Nuyorican Young Lords whose objective, like that of the Black Panther Party, was to gain 'community control over our institutions and land'.[11] A dozen blocks south, members of the mostly white, informally organized group COLAB, or Collaborative Projects, illegally entered an empty, city-owned building in the early hours of New Year's Day 1980. Inside, they set up a temporary exhibition entitled *The Real Estate Show*, before the NYPD padlocked it two days later, tossing much of the art out into the street. Surprisingly, subsequent negotiations with the city led to the formation of ABC No Rio art center, a collectively managed focal point for community activism and the punk scene thereafter, perhaps indicating just how devalued the city's real estate had become at the time.[12]

The influence of this DIY and counter-institutional activism on the mainstream art world began to show in June 1980 with *The Times Square Show* – a sprawling, haphazard exhibition installed in a former massage parlor that the *Village Voice* proclaimed as 'the first radical art show of the 1980s'.[13] The exhibition featured an admixture of youthful, graffiti-inspired works by Jean-Michel Basquiat and Keith Haring, contributions by street artists Jenny Holzer and John Ahearn, figurative paintings by 58-year-old art world apostate Leon Golub, and more. What *The Times Square Show* also announced in no uncertain terms was the end of Greenbergian era formalism. This chapter focuses on a couple of affiliated art collectives, Group Material (GM) and Political Art Documentation/Distribution (PAD/D), two explicitly activist, counter-institutional organizations with overlapping memberships, founded in 1979 and 1980 respectively. Significantly, these groups can be interpreted within the backstory of activist art in two contrasting ways: as constituting either a bridge leading back to the 1960s Left vanguard and its idealism, or a hinge swinging forward, linking to the emerging cultural paradigm of neoliberalism. Of course, neither analysis is without qualification or some degree of reductivism, but with those provisos in mind, I turn first to Group Material and its tactical orientation towards the contemporary artist as activist.

TACTICS, OR STRATEGIES?

Group Material's ardently radical manifesto proclaimed that it 'cannot possibly rely on winning validation from bright, white rooms and full-color repros in the art world glossies'. Instead, the informal 12-person collective sought to 'tap and promote the lived aesthetic of a largely "non-art" public – this is our goal, our contradiction, our energy'.[14] GM's practice in the early 1980s included meticulously designing curatorial projects that were featured in a storefront gallery on the Lower East Side. It was open 5–10 pm in order to accommodate working people, a policy that harkens back to the demands of AWC in 1969. The group's thematic exhibitions focused on such topics as alienation, gender, consumerism, food and fashion, always framed by a Marxian inspired analysis that was presented through display texts explicitly invoking Russian Constructivist typography. And rather than keep the walls of its experimental, not-for-profit gallery the standard, 'neutral' white, GM typically chose other colors, most often red. But along with the pedagogical tone, exhibitions also embraced pop cultural references in the form of vinyl album covers and store-bought items such as breakfast cereal boxes. As co-founder Tim Rollins explained GM's approach to aesthetics and collective decision-making, 'We got to bring to the table of collaboration whatever background we had, whatever baggage, whatever books we had read.'[15] If this was the reimagining of Russian vanguardism, it was being resurrected with a particularly pluralistic and American sensibility.

In early 1981 – about a year before leaving their 13th Street storefront space due to internal conflicts and financial challenges – Group Material organized one of its most memorable projects, *The People's Choice (Arroz con Mango)*. Overtly ethnographic, the unusual exhibition gathered everyday objects and images let to the group by its mostly Dominican and Puerto Rican neighbors. This included decorative ceramic plates, wedding photos, Caribbean toy dolls and a collection of animal-headed Pez candy dispensers accumulated by a local resident. *The People's Choice* sought to expose the false impartiality of the white cube gallery space and assumptions about what 'culture' was, and who it belonged to. It also reflected the all-white group's youthful, if inevitably handicapped, desire to escape such privileged shibboleths as formalist art and what they termed 'pseudo avant-gardism'.[16]

For art historian Alan Moore, *The People's Choice* exhibition was the culmination of the group members' search for 'discourse' beyond their own limited identities as 'artists'. With it, he writes, they realized an ambition shared by at least two other 1980s countercultural cultural spaces, ABC No Rio and Fashion Moda, which was to 'directly and effectively involve the community around the art gallery'.[17] But if Group Material's activist exhibition practice resolved for them, at least temporarily, the estranged condition of being an artist in an alienated capitalist society, PAD/D by contrast imagined its agency as stemming directly from communities excluded by the art world establishment, and towards a less and less invoked ideal of worldwide emancipation.

STRATEGIES RATHER THAN TACTICS

PAD/D operated out of a shared office in Lower Manhattan, in what was known as the Peace Pentagon due to the high number of Left and pacifist organizations housed inside its disintegrating edifice. The group's primary objective was to establish an archive of socially engaged art, in order to show by example

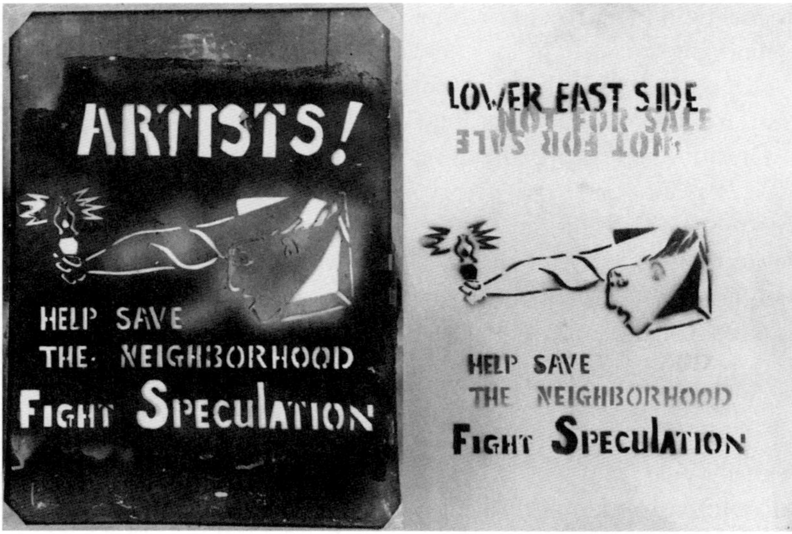

Fig.9 PAD/D (Political Art Documentation/Distribution) anti-gentrification street stencil by Michael Anderson, 1984, @gsholette.

how artists might directly support the radical transformative ideals of movements that thrived in decades past. PAD/D soon expanded its operations to include publishing the newsletter *UpFront*, creating art for political demonstrations, programming monthly presentations by marginalized performers and activists, often of color, and organizing a street-art campaign against the gentrification and displacement of long-term low-income residents on the Lower East Side.[18]

The group also produced what today would be labeled short-lived pop-up projects – including the exhibition *Death and Taxes*, for which artists created decentralized interventions in public spaces around New York City to protest government military spending, just before income taxes were due on 14 April – and fabricated art to be carried in demonstrations. Two examples of the latter are worth noting. For *Image War on the Pentagon*, a contingent of PAD/D members, carrying painted placards with crossed-out images of tanks and missiles, participated in the 1981 March against the Pentagon, a rally that drew 25,000 people – a substantial number considering that no US draft or war was taking place at the time. Similarly, in 1984, PAD/D members marched a 3 m-high inflatable Pac-Man wearing an Uncle Sam stars-and-stripes top hat through the city streets to protest at what appeared to be a pending invasion of Nicaragua and El Salvador by the Reagan administration (an all too familiar act of military meddling aimed at propping up endangered, decades-old, US-backed dictatorships). That same year the group participated in Artists' Call Against US Intervention in Central America, as mentioned in Chapter 1. This was arguably one of, if not the, last grassroots cultural protest campaign to mass-mobilize US artists in ways that resembled the art activism of the 1960s.

By the mid- to late-1980s, GM was shifting its approach regarding cultural activism, away from the streets and the public sphere, into such mainstream art exhibitions as the Whitney Biennial and documenta 8 in Kassel, Germany, both of which featured new commissioned projects by the collective. GM's argument was simple: more people would be exposed to the group's politically charged practice if it was legitimized by a major art world venue, rather than lost in a maze of urban spaces or marginalized in an alternative gallery. Bear in mind, this statement was made about a decade prior to the Internet becoming publicly accessible. All the same, GM continued to engage with progressive campaigns, including collaborating with CISPES, the Committee in Solidarity with the People of El Salvador, which was founded in 1980 in opposition to Ronald Reagan's support for right-wing and military regimes in Central America.

Meanwhile, PAD/D's primary aspiration remained largely unchanged: to link politically engaged artists to non-art-based social movements, with the goal of creating a truly alternative cultural commons, complete with its own autonomous sphere of progressive art. PAD/D's ambitious mission statement – inflected by groups such as AMCC, Red Herring, Amiri Baraka's Anti-Imperialist Cultural Union and even the Chicago Surrealists by way of the journal *Cultural Correspondence* – explicitly sought to build an 'international, grass roots network of artist/activists who will support with their talents and their political energies the liberation and self-determination of all disenfranchised peoples'.[19] As previously commented upon, this was indeed exorbitant and idealistic. And yet PAD/D's over-estimation was in keeping with decades of Black Liberation and anti-colonial struggles in the developing world. Still, by the early 1980s, the effectiveness of the New Left in the US had already been greatly compromised by undercover police and the covert FBI COINTELPRO program (1956–71) which engaged in surveillance, infiltration and disruption of domestic radical organizations. Correspondingly, a broader political shift was underway involving two factors. First was the election of the neo-conservative leaders Thatcher and Reagan whose policies stressed risk and entrepreneurship over social welfare. And second, artists were largely abandoning both Greenbergian formalism and Conceptualism, in order to expressively celebrate, rather than deconstruct, figurative representation and the spectacular imagery generated by television, cinema, pop music, advertising and fashion, but also street art, punk culture and graffiti. The popular success of this often amusingly entertaining, if intentionally low-brow, scene can be measured by the explosion of galleries, art biennials and record-breaking sales for the work of young artists, when compared to the visual austerity of the previous generation's art. The glitz of the 'GO GO '80s art world', as *ARTnews* described it, eclipsed even that of 1960s Pop art, and is perhaps best captured by this excerpt from a 1985 essay in the magazine:

> As artists become the subjects of increasing media hype, high visibility and upward mobility are defining their lives. What they wear and where they eat, live and play, as much as the art they make, are topics that attract the seemingly insatiable curiosity of a starstruck public.[20]

The initial stirrings of postwar art celebrity culture as presented by *Life* magazine's 1949 photospreads of all-American abstractionist Jackson Pollock, and later amplified by Andy Warhol's *Brillo Boxes* and floating *Silver Clouds* pillows was now turned-up full volume. Rather than the politicized heirs of Art Workers' Coalition, it was the groovy offspring of The Factory who came of age in the 1980s. Likewise, the exuberant discontent of the 1960s was replaced by inklings of a new economic effervescence that was not merely memorialized by avant-garde lifestyles, but now actually pivoted on the out-of-the-box audacity of risk-taking artistic labor. It would be another decade before the 1990 launch of the first web browser, the WorldWideWeb, and two decades more before the term 'creative economy' was minted by British media mogul John Howkins in 2001, but many of the elements leading to the total-social aestheticization of society can be traced back to the uninhibited confluence of art, fashion and capital that was manifest in the 1980s. This included the intensity and paradoxes of contemporary global high art, its multi-billion-dollar marketplace, duty-free ports and fine art equity markets, as well as the art of activism and the activism of art.

As Group Material sought to move practically, theoretically and artistically beyond the ever-diminishing zeitgeist of the 1968 'Great Refusal' by translating its engaged practice into an elastic cultural intervention targeting specific art world sites offered to the collective, PAD/D continued to anticipate the arrival of an emancipated 'people's culture' that required building an alternative political exhibition network, apart from the high art industry. Notably, Group Material's tactically oriented activism kept the collective running for almost two decades, compared with PAD/D's respectable but far shorter eight-year lifespan. More than that, Group Material's flexible style of working at both the margins and center of the art world established a conceptual stage for a new cohort of mid-1980s art collectives that were focused less on seeking broad political transformation or establishing a progressive alternative counter-culture, than on targeting highly specific social issues. Thus, the Guerrilla Girls' campaign to get equitable compensation and representation for women and people of color in the art world, and Gran Fury and DIVA TV's public countering of deceptive and homophobic government AIDS policies, paved the way for a host of new collectives that took shape over the next decade, as tactics displaced longer-term, strategic activism, particularly after the Cold War's end in 1991.[21] This new activist art repurposed the Situationist practice of *détournement* in order to carry out subversive acts of digital mimesis, guerilla media sabotage, and what the culture jamming activist duo Yes Men labeled corporate 'identity correction' – all interventions far better suited to the emerging era of visually saturated cyberspace than to the post-1960s New Left.[22]

And yet, as much as the spirit of ultra-free market enterprise culture engulfs dissident social organizing and identity, turning resistance into an individual subjective rather than a collective political experience, it also exposes itself to the possibility of new forms of opposition, now relocated within its very core. Thus, new types of confrontation and withdrawal take advantage of the system's flexible networks, tactics and technologies. There is, in short, a specter haunting the spectacle. It is motivated by the dream of unfettered artistic agency, direct democracy and the end of racialized, gendered and sexual oppression, as proposed by social movements in the 1960s, 1970s and 1980s. And for a brief, vertiginous moment in the 1990s, this liberated creativity seemed almost within reach, thanks to the ethereal realm of digital communalism that gave birth to a new type of art activism known as tactical media.

Chapter 8

1990s: Repurposing Situationism as Tactical Media

'Digital technology could enable an extraordinary range of ordinary people to become part of a creative process.'[1]
Lawrence Lessig

'Being neither cute nor ugly, good or bad, tactical media appear, strike and disappear again. Instead of the old school rituals of negation and refusal, tactical media engage both makers and users, producers and viewers, into a game of appearances and disappearances.'[2]
Geert Lovink

In 1997, buoyed by the seemingly borderless territory opened up by digital and cellular communications technologies, two media theorists, Geert Lovink and David Garcia, produced a new manifesto for a new medium. 'The ABC of Tactical Media' was not plastered on walls or dropped from a plane, as the 'Manifesto of Futurism' was in 1909, but uploaded on Friday 16 May to an independent Internet mailing list called Nettime .org. It had been six years since the collapse of the USSR and six years too since the release of the first Internet browser, WorldWideWeb. With Soviet-style socialism being replaced by Western-style democracy – a process that some labeled 'political normalization' – neolibertarian thinkers like Lawrence Lessig foresaw an emerging, digitally linked global society brimming with freewheeling entrepreneurial creativity and exchange, while the political theorist Francis Fukuyama famously asserted

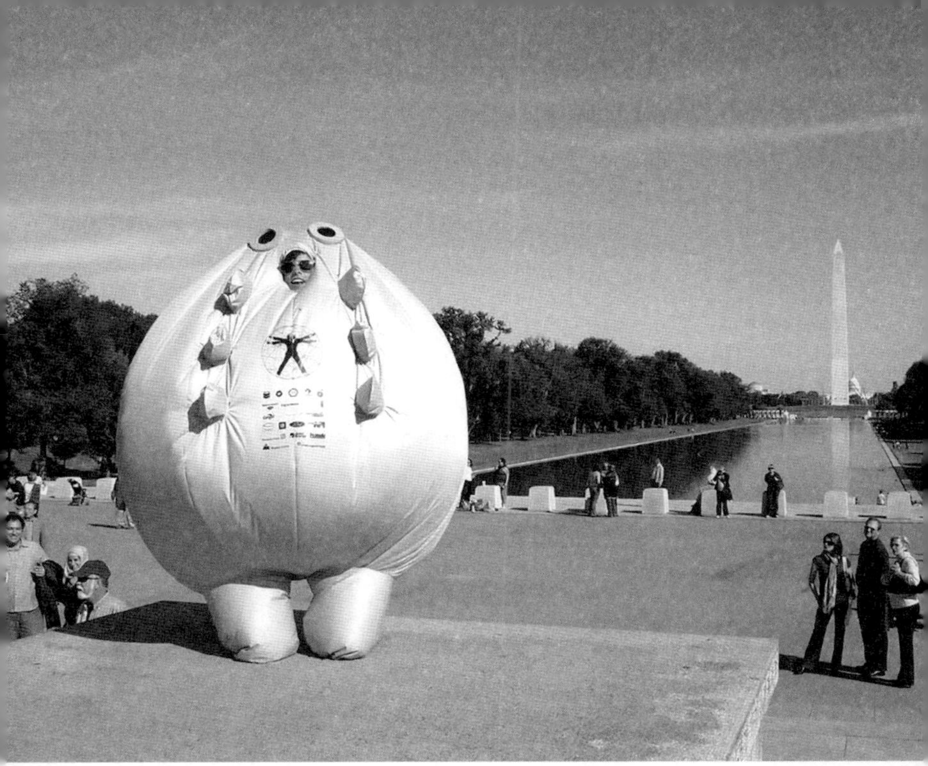

Fig.10 The Yes Men's *Survivaball* allegedly invented by the global terra-forming corporation Halliburton in the wake of Hurricane Katrina. The high-tech, disaster-resistant garment is inflated by a CEO or CFO in the event of future natural disasters amplified by fossil-fuel-driven climate change. Photo courtesy of The Yes Men.

that history itself had at long last reached an end, as liberal capitalism achieved hegemony over all other ideologies.[3]

No less enthused by promises of political and technological transformation, Lovink and Garcia were nevertheless skeptical that a cyber version of Adam Smith's 'invisible hand' would lead to anything other than a corporate-dominated online marketplace. Seeking instead to radically reimagine post-1968 cultural politics, they called for tactical media (TM) to carry out a Situationist *détournement* of capital's society of the spectacle, only now via 'cheap "do it yourself" media, made possible by the revolution in consumer electronics and expanded forms of distribution'.[4] Grafting the direct visual activism of groups such as ACT UP, Gran Fury, DIVA TV, the Guerrilla Girls and older models such as Augusto Boal's 1970s The Theater of the Oppressed onto the theories of Michel de Certeau's *The Practice of Everyday Life*, Lovink and Garcia championed an aesthetic made up of 'clever tricks, the hunter's cunning, maneuvers, polymorphic situations, joyful discoveries, poetic as well as warlike'.[5] This new art activist tendency rejoiced in immediate, agile tactics as opposed to strategic, long-term planning. They illustrated their thesis by citing the artist Krzysztof Wodiczko's mobile homeless shelter units and public projections focused on giving agency to nomadic urban populations, insisting that 'the hunted must discover the ways of becoming the hunter'.[6] For Lovink and Garcia, TM was all about 'the temporary connections you are able to make. Here and now, not some vaporware promised for the future. But what we can do on the spot with the media we have access to.'[7]

AVANT-GARDE REDUX?

For scholar Gavin Grindon, this new wave of cultural activism, especially in its urban interventionist form such as Take Back the Streets and Yomango, seemed like a second wave of Situationism, while Yates McKee adopted the term 'Neo-Situationism', though in a more ambiguous way in order to both identify and critique TM.[8] Undoubtedly, this new and nimble form of tactical protest culture constituted an iteration of collective agency that was sharply different from the dominant progressive politics of preceding decades. For however much the extra-parliamentary activism of the New Left differed from the grand ambitions of earlier mass parties, groups as diverse as the Black Panthers, Young Lords, New Communist Movement, urban squatters, feminist anti-war occupiers, activist art collectives like PAD/D and Amiri Barka's Anti-Imperialist Cultural Union, all desired to establish genuine autonomy from the tyranny of racialized capitalism, defunded cities, patriarchy and even the art world marketplace. By contrast, TM presented itself not as a set of beliefs or any type of politics, utopian or otherwise, but instead as an intangible force whose fleeting maneuvers actively tried to invert normal expectations as a form of interruption or intervention. More Dadaist than Constructivist oriented, in Lovink and Garcia's terms, this weak form of resistance holds no political ground because 'whatever it wins, it does not keep' and since it is only realized situationally, while 'on the wing', it also has 'no image of itself'.[9]

Thus, for TM, the poor, working class, women, people of color and LGBTQ people did not represent unique and ontologically privileged political subjects of social and historical transformation. Instead, all these subjugated populations constituted a multitude, as posited by political theorists Antonio Negri and Michael Hardt, an amalgamation of forces 'from below' whose self-valorization and collective experimentation – made possible above all by the Internet – hold out the unique promise of realizing new forms of social agency.[10] By eschewing traditional party formations for self-empowerment, the multitude represents an aesthetic force rather than a strictly political agency, as Michael Denning argues and as I discussed in the previous chapter.[11]

Going one step further, the cultural theorist Brian Holmes maintains that TM activated the multitude's 'radically democratic desire that could be summed up in a seemingly impossible phrase: do-it-yourself geopolitics'.[12] Which is to say, digital technology provided everyone with a set of accessible tools that not only permitted cutting and pasting existing images and sound recordings into new configurations, but also meant that anyone could initiate their own new music label, independent art gallery, autonomous university or activist movement, including, admittedly, the speculative far right conspiratorial universe of QAnon, whose cyberbirth was still more than a decade away. If geopolitics had always been a game played between states, mass parties and politicians, it now suddenly appeared accessible to the multitude via culture, as evidenced by the digital interventionist projects of Electronic Disturbance Theater (EDT), Ultra Red and Critical Art Ensemble (CAE), but also Reclaim the Streets in the UK, the Zapatista rebellion in Mexico, and of course later with Occupy Wall Street in 2011, or later still with voluntary Ukrainian cyberdefense 'hacker' corps digitally undermining Russian military communications in 2022.[13] But tactical media also made fully discernible the demise of mass politics that had been underway since at least the flatlining of 1968, a process that favored an activism which mobilized everyday moments of microresistance over group identity formation and unified mass struggle. What was less immediately obvious at the time perhaps, was the degree to which TM's neo-Situationist aesthetic benefited from the post-Cold War capitalist hegemony of radically deregulated, crossborder investment, as well as the 1993 founding of the European Union, a new political entity that pumped massive funding into programs like Creative Europe and rotating Capitals of Culture. Where capital goes, so follows art, even if it does so oppositionally, or at best, ambiguously.

NEO-SITUATIONISM

Contemporary artists from the 1980s onwards found themselves courted by an expanding circuit of newly minted museums, *Kunsthalles*, art centers, public festivals and cultural conferences. These organizations took an interest in political and activist art practitioners. But there is another, differing contrast between TM and previous generations: while earlier activist art groups such as Art Workers' Coalition, Artists Meeting for Cultural Change,

Black Mask and Hackney Flashers all wrestled with issues of co-optation by the mainstream, TM ploughed directly, even gleefully, into the sphere of mass-media machinations, but did so with a critical twist by temporarily occupying and subverting the message of the electronic medium. A 1998 communique by RTMark (soon to become The Yes Men) explains how its activist tactics use 'the effects and strength of corporations, the strength they have arrogated over the years, to unseat them and to attack them'.[14] By contrast, consider the agonized self-analysis and *mea culpa* from a 1977 editorial in the Marxist-oriented Left art journal *Red Herring*: 'There may be little we can do to stop this magazine from becoming another coffee-table class diversion,' (though they pledged to see 'that isn't all it becomes').[15]

Once an attack is over, TM practitioners move on to a new target, generating different avatars and cover personas in the process. Between the early 1990s and 2021, Igor Vamos and Jacques Servin, the constituent members of RTMark and The Yes Men, have changed identities many times, using, abandoning and sometimes then reusing such *noms de guerre* as Mike Bonanno, Andy Bichlbaum, Ernesto Lucha, Ray Thomas and Frank or Fransisco Guerrero, among others, all adopted in order to carry out the 'identity correction' of socially offensive corporations and government authorities. One of their most audacious détournements began by mimicking Dow Chemical Company's website, leading an unsuspecting BBC reporter to interview the group in 2003. Servin arrived at the BBC taping session masquerading as a Dow spokesperson named Jude Finisterra, a preposterous merger of St Jude, patron of lost causes, with *finisterra*, a word meaning 'end of the earth' in Latin.

Broadcasting to millions of viewers, Finisterra announced that the American company was going to provide unprecedented financial compensation to the survivors and families of the Union Carbide gas leak in Bhopal India, a disaster that had killed almost 4000 people 20 years earlier.[16] Dow Chemical's stock lost some US$2 billion in value before The Yes Men were outed for their hijacking, leaving the company's real spokespeople in the awkward position of having to publicly state that no justice would be provided to the injured population of Bhopal after all. The group thus leveraged the power of the corporation against itself, at least in terms of mass-media visibility.

Still, while appropriation, intervention, culture jamming and what McKenzie Wark called 'hacktivism' defined the activist art of the 1990s and early 2000s, thus reimagining 1960s Situationism by way of digital or digitally assisted media, TM also reveals two significant inconsistencies of relevance to the arguments in this book.[17] The first anomaly involves the use of handcraft practices transformed into an activist media, the second is the curious emergence of ersatz para-institutions during the 1990s that on the surface appear to contradict TM's 'hold no ground' ethos. For although the practice of TM was dominated by digital software and occasionally hardware – and sometimes even wetware, as in biologically oriented art projects – the 1990s were also marked by the emergence of Craftivism: protest art practices involving techniques associated with women's labor, such as needlework, crocheting and quilting, all now repurposed for social critique. One example is Marianne Jørgensen's enormous, collaboratively quilted pink tea cozy (2006) that completely enveloped a military tank in Denmark, to signify popular opposition to the country's involvement in the US-led occupation of Iraq. A similar knit cocooning the *Charging Bull* sculpture on Wall Street in 2010 is discussed in Chapter 8. Craftivism may appear to be an anomaly in the era of tactical media, but as we shall see it represents a significant development towards the most current forms of protest aesthetics.

MOCKSTITUTIONS

TM ran parallel to, and was fueled by, the counter-globalization campaigns with the motto 'another world is possible' that arose in the 1990s in opposition to neoliberalism. It claimed a particular fidelity to the Indigenous Zapatista rebellion, a horizontally structured, decolonial movement in Chiapas, Mexico, which made use of the early Internet to mobilize opposition against the North American Free Trade Agreement, among other targets.

Despite TM's stated platform of remaining in constant flux, the affinity with the Zapatistas suggests that even the most ephemeral, de-territorialized and tactical forms of art activism harbor hopes of establishing a distributed form of alternative governance in a radically transformed social terrain – a notion implicit in Holmes's idea of DIY geopolitics. This impulse might also explain the common TM practice of inventing faux institutions, which Belarusian artist Marina Naprushkina labels 'artificial institutions', and Carrie Lambert-Beatty calls 'para-fictional institutions'.[18] I assign the neologism 'mockstitution' in order to underscore the typically acerbic stance towards formal organizing that most of the examples exhibited, at least in their early stages.

The 1990s was a decade that gave rise to an unprecedented throng of pseudonymous institutes, leagues, schools, bureaus, centers, offices, departments, corporations, societies, clubs and even a church presided over by performance artist/preacher Reverend Billy. Each mockstitution sported an authentic-looking website, mission statement and logo, as though TM's tactics of constant plasticity could only be allowed to stabilize in the form of a counterfeit identity, even to the point of patent exaggeration. These playfully invented organizations served as command posts for Situationist-inspired activism, but they also substituted their own fictional mediating functions for actual social institutions that were vanishing under pro-market neoliberal policies. In point of fact, many mockstitutions ultimately performed as well as, or even better than, the authentic structures that they impersonated or lampooned.

TM's many para-institutional entities included San Francisco's Center for Tactical Magic, which mixed art with witchcraft while employing 'disguise, humour, surprise', writes the researcher Gretchen Coombs, in order to disrupt 'our understanding of what can happen in public space'.[18] Similarly, the Church of Stop Shopping, Office for Anti-Propaganda and Laboratory of Insurrectionary Imagination (with its rebel clown army and experimental permaculture farm) operated in physical spaces, but added wobble and doubt to everyday life by performing a proxy version of the real world. More technology-oriented mockstitutions included the Carbon Defense League, Institute for Applied Autonomy and the aforementioned CAE and EDT, all of whom specialized in creative hacking, online culture jamming and reverse engineering both software and hardware in an attempt to make such technology more democratically accessible and less corporately monopolized.

In the early 2000s in Barcelona, the conspicuously neo-Situationist collective *Las Agencias* launched a line of activist street wearables in vibrant, if not clownish, colors that concealed internal body armor made from filled water bottles to repel blows from police batons. Reborn a few years later as Yomango – or 'I steal' in Spanish – the transformed group modified its garments to make them less conspicuous, but with similar secret pockets meant to confront the economic precarity of neoliberalism by using the 'five-finger discount', also known as shoplifting. 'You want it? You got it!' assured the group's slogan, clearly inspired by Situationist and student graffiti from Paris, 1968. Facsimile franchises of the Yomango brand soon popped up in other countries, including Germany, Mexico, Chile and Argentina.

TM, along with other activist art practices discussed in this book, has frequently engaged in acts of repurposing and reactivating cultural forms, ideas, methods and events mined from the surplus archive from below. The mockstitution is itself a type of reuse activism. I might even go so far as to propose that practices of artistic recycling have become as important as, or provide a substitution for, the customary avant-garde aspiration towards conceptual and formal originality. Indeed, procedures of recovery and reinterpretation have become central to contemporary protest culture and, in what we might think of as archival *détournement* in which past content now absent or embargoed from public space is recovered and re-animated in the present (more on this idea ahead).

For example, between 2007 and 2008, Howling Mob Society illegally installed official-looking metal street signs around downtown Pittsburgh that narrated the little-known history of the city's 1877 Great Railroad Strike. In 2001–2 in Southern

California, the Pochx Research Society of Erased and Invisible Histories (Sandra de la Loza) fastened metal plaques to public monuments in order to illuminate aspects of the region's suppressed Chicanx and Latinx past, and in 2008 marked the site of a whitewashed 1932 mural by the Leftist Mexican artist David Alfaro Siqueiros.[20] Both Howling Mob and Pochx Research Society followed the work of the NYC collective REPOhistory, which in 1992 obtained a one-year permit from the Department of Transportation (under David Dinkins, the city's first Black mayor) to install site-specific street signs that 'repossessed' and decolonized local histories. The project countermanded the quincentennial celebrations of Christopher Columbus, alleged 'discoverer of the new world', with images and texts detailing the stories of non-white, working-class, leftist and unhoused peoples. Two years later, REPOhistory followed up with *Queer Spaces*, a series of triangular pink street signs marking sites of historical significance to the gay, lesbian and trans communities, including the approximate location where the queer liberation activist Marsha P. Johnson was last seen alive prior to her 1992 death, which may have been a hate-crime murder and is still under investigation.[21]

REPOhistory's final street sign project, however, was met with opposition. It included work by Jenny Polak and David Thorne detailing police violence against young people of color, including murders, as well as a piece by Marina Gutierrez, accusing the city of racism. Before it could go up, the installation was stopped cold by the four-year old administration of Republican Mayor Rudolph Giuliani, who refused to provide the group with a permit. Only after REPOhistory and public interest lawyers organized a successful legal challenge to the city's sudden and arbitrary new policy governing public space did it proceed as planned.

THE FALL OF TACTICAL MEDIA

Yet the openness and accessibility to art activists of actual urban streets and cyberspace was beginning to come to an end by the late 1990s, as local processes of gentrification, and national and international systems of regulation and surveillance, started to transform or terminate TM's relatively unrestricted practice of carrying out politically charged aesthetic interventions. Perhaps no incident underscores the nature of this shift better than the absurd bioterrorist case brought against the group Critical Art Ensemble. In 2002, working in collaboration with artists Beatriz da Costa and Claire Pentecost, CAE attempted to develop botanically interventionist countermeasures against the genetically modified plant seeds of corporate agribusiness Monsanto. Two years later, the group's cofounder Steve Kurtz was being charged with bioterrorism by the US government under George W. Bush – extravagant accusations that were only finally dismissed in 2008, though not before a pall was cast over TM in general. Adding to the notoriety of neo-Situationism was FloodNet, a Distributed denial of service (DDoS) software program developed in 1997 by Ricardo Dominguez and EDT as a means of staging non-violent, electronic sit-ins. Inspired by the Italian Strano Network's previous virtual strike in 1993, EDT intended to target the website of the Mexican government, in order to demonstrate support for the Zapatista uprising. Engaging in similar work in the next decade, members of the online hacktivist network Anonymous were arrested in 2013 for a DDoS attack on PayPal after the company refused to process payments to WikiLeaks, the classified media news platform. PayPal alleged it lost over US$5 million during the assault.[22]

Especially after the terrorist attacks of 2001 and the 2008–9 economic meltdown, TM's seemingly unbridled horizon of operations began to contract. Along the way, though, other Situationist-inspired revival projects took root, including direct, embodied interventions in the neoliberal cityscape, as a wave of occupations swept many capitals and forced a rethinking of the aspirations and limits of digitized cultural activism. Now under increasing duress, the line separating art activism from activism per se begins its real dissolution, as cultural protest practices become entangled with actual legal confrontations, a tendency that has only accelerated into the 2020s.

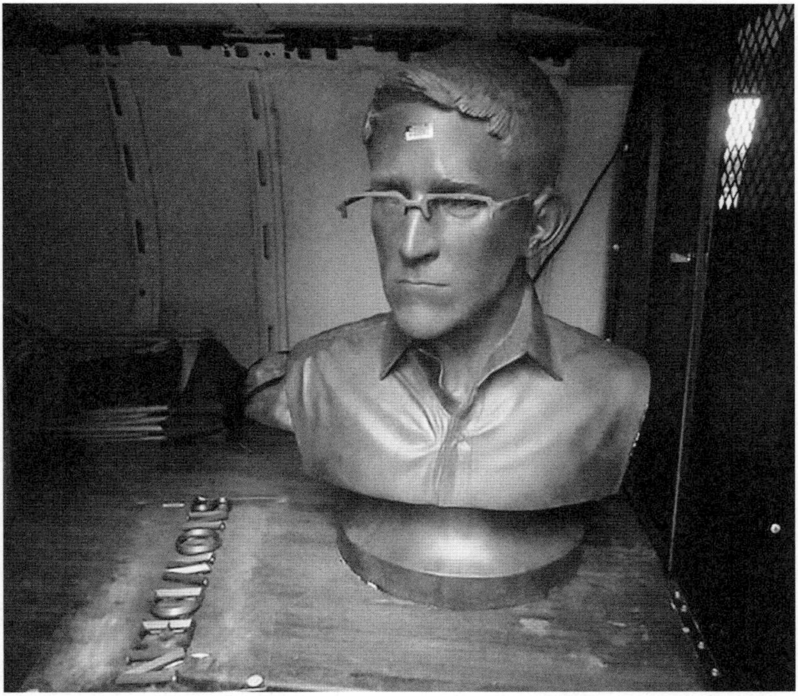

Fig.11 Artists Jeff Greenspan and Andrew Ticer created a sculptural bust of government surveillance whistleblower Edward Snowden and covertly installed their faux monument in Fort Greene Park, Brooklyn, NY, late at night on 6 April 2015. Here the work is seen being returned to the artists by the Parks Department, along with a US$50 fine for illegal park entry. Photo courtesy Jeff Greenspan and Andrew Ticer.

Chapter 9

Back to the Streets: From Tactical Media to Occupy Wall Street (2011)

> 'When talking about it afterwards, everyone tends to stress the same thing: the experience of autonomy, the opportunity, even if only for a moment, to occupy a space not under Their Control, in which the only rules are those generated collectively, by the group.'[1]
> *David Graeber*

Towards the end of the 21st century's first decade, another shift became evident, not only in the methods of art activism, but also in the spaces where it operated and the expectations for what it might accomplish. Several broader changes precipitated this restructuring. At the same time that the Left counter-global movement began to dissolve, the state ramped up the security and surveillance measures it imposed on the general population, both outcomes of the 9/11 terrorist attacks in the US as well as bombings and public assaults in Russia, Spain, England, Nigeria, Iraq and other countries. This marked the beginning of a different type of anti-globalization critique from that of the Left. If the counter-globalization movement hoped for a borderless but also postcapitalist world, the new Right-leaning anti-globalists were in favor of a highly nationalistic capitalism that re-established borders to seemingly protect against mostly imagined enemies based on ethnicity, religion, skin color and, in the 2020s, viral infection. Meanwhile, the wild cyberspace frontier in which Al-Qaeda had indeed recruited some of its

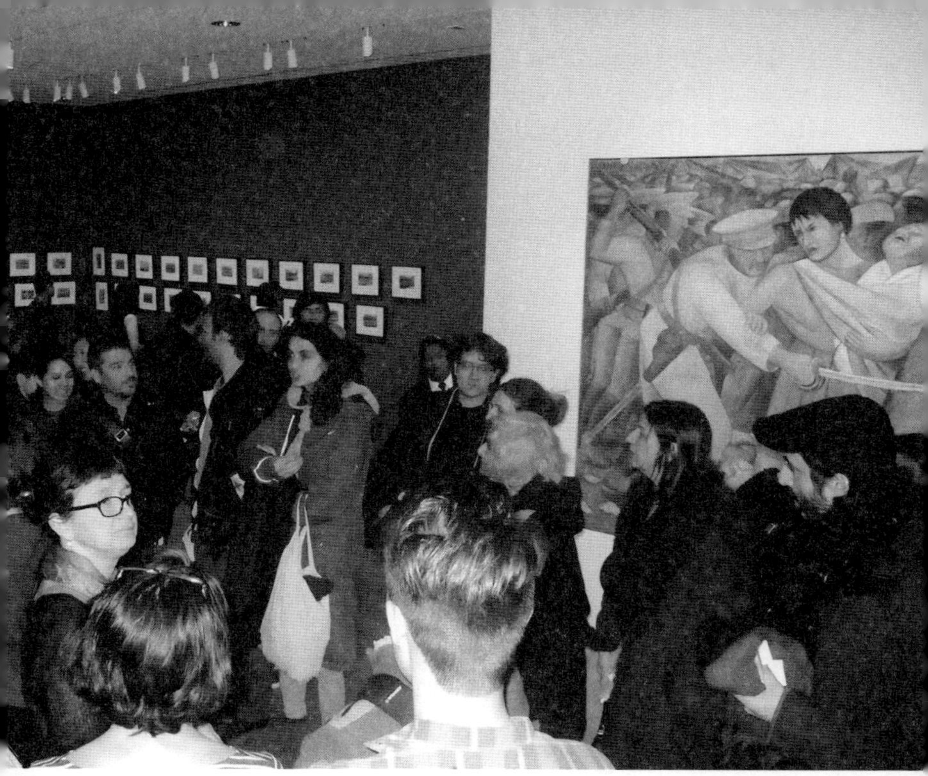

Fig.12 One of many sub-groups that emerged during Occupy Wall Street is Occupy Museums, seen here entering the Museum of Modern Art's *Diego Rivera* exhibition *en masse* on 14 January 2012, where they held a mic-check general assembly about Rivera's Leftist politics and museum board members linked with profiting from crippling consumer and student debt. Photo courtesy of Noah Fischer and Occupy Museums.

electronic jihadists was being increasingly fenced in by legal statutes like the USA Patriot Act, a measure that amplified existing laws, including criminalizing virtual distributed-denial-of-service sit-ins like those of EDT's FloodNet.[2]

RESISTANCE ABHORS AN ASPIRATIONAL VACUUM

State measures after September 11 2001 worked to tighten rules against protest actions like CAE's anti-Monsanto 'fuzzy biological sabotage' that targeted genetically altered seed grains, stopping just short of redefining this type of militant cultural activism as 'terrorism'. All the while, monolithic corporations began monetizing cyberspace by locking up content that had previously flowed freely online, while developing new types of value extraction from that content, astonishing even for capitalism. This involved mining and monetizing not only data, but attention spans, shared content and emotional experiences that many began giving to the corporate sector freely without compensation via platforms such as Facebook. Situationist fears of a mass alienating spectacle were morphing into the direct financialization of consciousness. Capitalism had discovered a new golden goose, and it was algorithmic.

Direct digital democracy did not die under these circumstances but it was deflated, and then reanimated as an array of subscriber services. Although still internally horizontal to some degree, the Internet was fast becoming disconnected from any lingering promise of an open source, global infrastructure in which everyone could share their unbridled creativity. Then in 2008 came the cold, gray reality of a jobless future, brought about by a massive, global financial meltdown. Between roughly 2007 and 2009, an estimated US$8–12 trillion of value vanished from capitalist coffers worldwide. Severe austerity measures soon followed, as nations around the world forced citizens, a global majority already living in precarious conditions, into still greater positions of risk (while providing profitable extraction opportunities to the wealthy). The largest economic crash since the Great Depression of the 1930s swept away the giddy, emancipatory expectations of the 'creative class', a term for intellectual workers proposed by neoliberal management guru Richard Florida.[3]

Although most artists lost whatever slim stability they had marshaled prior to the collapse, it was also a moment of political awakening for cultural workers as they came face-to-face with their own insecurity, now minus the airy concoctions of the creative economy. In the US in particular, many confronted substantial art school debt – individual financial obligations averaging tens of thousands of dollars. Artists also began to recognize the similar precariousness faced by other semi- and unemployed laborers and this moment of political awakening was unquestionably a factor in the current eruption of art activism which gave rise to this book.

OCCUPY EVERYTHING (AND WHAT COMES AFTER)

Within a few years, protest occupations in urban spaces had spread from city to city, starting in the Middle East in 2010, followed by Spain, the US and then seemingly everywhere around the globe. The occupations congealed first in ancient plazas in Tunisia with the self-immolation of Mohamed Bouazizi, unemployed after authorities confiscated his modest street-vending wares. From there, uprisings began in Tahrir Square in Egypt, followed by Yemen, Libya, Syria and other nearby nations. Although focused initially on basic demands for jobs, dignity and bread, the urban rebellions soon expanded to include demands for revolutionary social change and the toppling of authoritarian regimes. Once Puerta del Sol, Madrid, was occupied by anti-austerity protesters, it seemed as if an unstoppable human swarm of *indignados*, invisibles and the aggrieved had been released on the world, including across Europe, into Russia and Hong Kong, as well as over the ocean where occupiers descended on a privatized city park near Wall Street at the bottom of Manhattan. The swarm in the United States consisted largely of former creative workers whose futures had been put on indefinite hold by the so-called new normal, an economy that would never revert to its pre-2008 state. With ever-growing numbers, the occupiers chanted, 'We are the 99 per cent', spotlighting their precarious situation, and resonating with interventions around the world symbolically, and literally, as tweets and envoys traveled from Tahrir and Madrid to New York and back again. Occupy Wall Street (OWS), with substantial encampments in Washington, D.C., Boston, Chicago, Oakland, Portland and many smaller cities – established itself as counter-cultural shantytowns overflowing with impromptu, anti-capitalist speeches, DIY music, dance and art, improvised messages scrawled on the back of pizza delivery boxes, a people's library (in Zuccotti Park) and a reverberating, non-electronic, person-to-person voice-amplification system known as the 'human mic'. Simultaneously, this new generation of activist occupiers put their bodies 'on the line' while also taking advantage of Wi-Fi and cellular networks by employing digital services like Twitter and Facebook – technologies that had not been available to counter-globalization demonstrators in Seattle and elsewhere just over a decade earlier. They seamlessly embodied and livestreamed their occupation via both real and virtual space

In this sense, OWS salvaged some residual but nonetheless key elements of tactical media's techtopian promise. In the words of the theorist Marco Baravalle, co-founder of S.a.L.E. Docks cultural center in Venice, Italy, which began in 2007 as a squat occupation of an abandoned salt warehouse in Dorsoduro, 'today artists are again imagining alternative futures starting from a materialistic critique of the present'.[4] Which is to say that out of concrete conditions and altered historical circumstances, artists began thinking again of long-term solutions; mere mock institutions grew into or were replaced by 'alter-institutionality', (Baravalle's term) as cultural organizing took place in-between governmental institutions, the Internet and spaces of relative autonomy. In this sense, OWS repurposed not so much the 'cunning, maneuvers, polymorphic situations' of TM's neo-Situationism, but rather its appetite for establishing para-fictitious agencies to serve as operational platforms for hacks, pranks and public interventions. OWS might be thought of, therefore, as the ultimate mockstitution, like a tactically organized city in miniature, or a ghost city suddenly materializing within the bowels of a real metropolis, which it then proceeded to haunt, day in and day out, in every imaginable way, first by refusing to leave Zuccotti Park and then by refusing to provide the authorities with a set of demands that would, if somehow ever met, presumably bring about an end to the occupation. OWS was an uninvited poltergeist agency, thriving and momentarily dominating the aesthetics of the mass spectacle, thanks in large part to its own improbability.

The art associated with OWS is similarly phantasmic in nature, sometimes consisting of digitally streamed assemblies, lectures, discussions or performances that originated in Zuccotti Park, at other times manifesting as direct tactical actions, like the illegal yarn-bomb attack carried out by the Polish, New York-based artist Olek at around 3 am on Christmas morning in 2010. It was in fact a few months before the start of the occupation when, prophetically, she managed to encase Wall Street's iconic *Charging Bull* sculpture completely in a form-fitting, hand-crocheted cocoon. Olek's fluorescent pink-and-blue intervention shimmered in what looked like digital pixelation, offering a wry, if short-lived commentary on the vanishing effect of financialized capital. Before sun-up, authorities had cut away the bull's suit. Yet Olek's action remains intact as a digitally archived image that is frequently reproduced in relationship to OWS. The image functions as a metaphor for the encampment's two-fold seizure of physical and cyber realities, a fitting archetype for the activist art to come.

WAGES FOR ART WORKERS?

On 15 November 2011, police emptied Zuccotti Park of occupiers. The people's park was then power-scrubbed, its library, gray-water treatment experiments, cooking facilities and media stations hurriedly packed up and moved, or trashed. But the occupying swarms of precarious 99 per centers added vital momentum to existing, post-2008 art collectives in search of art world economic justice – among them W.A.G.E. (Working Artists and the Greater Economy), BFAMFAPhD, Liberate Tate and Gulf Labor Coalition (GLC) – while generating a host of new groups inspired by Occupy's aesthetic of communal assembly, including Arts & Labor, Occupy Museums and Debtfair. In the UK, Liberate Tate carried out six years of performative interventions between 2010 and 2016, to protest against British Petroleum's (BP) corporate sponsorship of the Tate museums; the group's actions included dousing a volunteer with thick tar-like goo inside one of the institutions and marching an enormous wind turbine 'gift' into Tate Modern's famed Turbine Hall to highlight non-fossil fuel energy alternatives.[5] And while Tate has never acknowledged the influence of this direct art activist campaign, it finally announced an end to its affiliation with BP in 2016.

Similarly, although with less of a conclusive outcome, Gulf Labor Coalition and its offshoot Global Ultra Luxury Faction (GULF) protested against the Guggenheim Museum's planned Abu Dhabi facility over the United Arab Emirates' unfair treatment of its large migrant construction-worker population (fig.14). Human Rights Watch described the labor conditions as seriously exploitative, with internal critics of the regime being silenced by lengthy imprisonment.[6] GLC and GULF first boycotted and publicly chastised the museum in 2010, before eventually occupying both the corporation's flagship Fifth Avenue location in New York and the Peggy Guggenheim Collection in Venice. In 2017, work was paused on the new Frank Gehry designed museum structure in Abu Dhabi, as members of GLC and GULF were themselves put under surveillance and later blocked from entry into the UAE, 'for security reasons'.[7]

Labor issues also emerged in the Western world after the 2008 financial crash. The group W.A.G.E. sought to regulate and guarantee artist fees in the US, while offering certification for cooperating nonprofit art organizations. One of the group's slogans, 'We Demand Payment for Making the World More Interesting', seemingly inverted the Situationist objective of wholesale creative liberation that prompted everybody to 'Take Your Desires for Reality'.[8] Given over 30 years of neoliberal ascendancy, it is not all that surprising to find a certain capitalist realism prevailing, even among the art world's precarious workless workers. Likewise, Occupy Museums, Debtfair and Arts & Labor have all sought to end exploitative cultural labor practices, whether by supporting striking Sotheby's art handlers or calling for a debt jubilee to forgive an average estimated US$32,731 of student loans per individual in 2015.[9] When challenged about how to pay for increased wages, better cultural working conditions and debt forgiveness, activists have pointed to a US$50 billion and rising art market (down 22 percent from 2019 due to COVID-19), with Sotheby's auction house raking in over 13 million in sales of contemporary art in one evening on 12 May 2020 alone. Considering the state of the larger world, it was perhaps inevitable that activists after 2008 began to focus on this decidedly financialized, though increasingly unconcealed, or 'bare' art world, seeking social justice within its institutional architecture. But an unexpected pivot happened when resistance against art world precariousness took hold deeper inside the esteemed citadels of high culture.

Chapter 10

Institutional Critique or Cultural Abolition?

> 'There is no document of civilization which is not at the same time a document of barbarism. And just as such a document is not free of barbarism, barbarism taints also the manner in which it was transmitted from one owner to another.'[1]
> *Walter Benjamin*

> 'Art activists do want to be useful, to change the world, to make the world a better place – but at the same time, they do not want to cease being artists.'[2]
> *Boris Groys*

In early 2019, dozens of lower-ranking staff members at New York City's New Museum announced their intention to form a labor union in search of better pay and benefits, but also greater respect from management. Although the late curator Marcia Tucker founded the museum in 1977 with a highly experimental and progressive mission, its 21st-century neoliberalized upper management hired a 'union avoidance' firm to thwart employees' organizing efforts. The workers nevertheless voted to become the New Museum Union, joining the United Auto Workers union Local 2110, which also represents the Museum of Modern Art's staff union that had organized in 1971 during the heady art activist epoch of AWC, GAAG and MBGC, as discussed in Chapter 4. But in 2019, the success of the New Museum staff unionization leapt like a grassfire to the Guggenheim and the

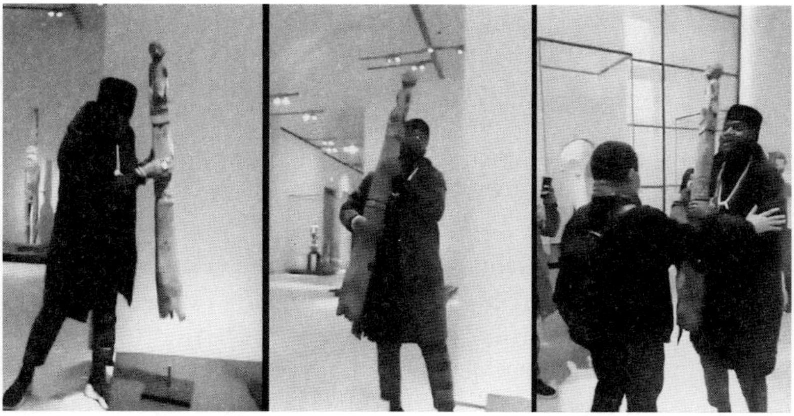

Fig.13 'I came here to take back what was stolen and plundered from us ... to take back what was pillaged from Africa,' tweeted Congolese activist Emery Mwazulu Diyabanza, after removing a 9th-century Chadian wooden funerary post from the Musée du Quai Branly in Paris, 22 October 2020. Screen grab composites from online Facebook video, @gsholette.

Whitney museums, and then to cultural institutions across the nation. In early 2022, the museum unionization wave continued to accelerate, even as many culture industry layoffs take place, which senior management blamed on the economic slowdown from the COVID-19 pandemic. In March, Whitney Museum staff boldly confronted VIP Biennial guests over their as yet unmet demands.

Especially noteworthy is that many of these lower echelon museum employees are also graduates of higher educational art programs in the visual arts and art history. All of which raises the intriguing possibility that 50-some years after it was introduced, the concept of institutional critique may be coming home to roost.[3] Only this time, the critique is spreading amongst those tasked with literally keeping the museum running: art handlers hanging canvases and constructing exhibition walls, curatorial assistants writing press releases, wait-staff serving lattes and biscotti in cafes, janitors cleaning bathroom stalls and mopping floors, and guards keeping multimillion-dollar objects secure within white cube citadels. Unlike institutionally critical artists, these are the essential cultural workers who operate invisibly within plain sight. Significantly, this campaign of internal institutional critique and labor organizing is conjoined with a robust external protest movement that has parallel objectives, including the removal of so-called 'toxic' board members with ties to industries that pollute, profit from personal debt, and from opioid and military products. It is also important to point out here that other protest demands go much further, including the proposition of abolishing high cultural institutions altogether.

THIS IS NOT YOUR GRANDPARENTS' INSTITUTIONAL CRITIQUE

If this is indeed a return of institutional critique, then it is applying art historical lessons in a truly novel way. Rather than creating exhibitable projects that aesthetically deconstruct museum spaces or that peel back high culture's ideological facade – as was the case with such pioneers of the field as Michael Asher, Daniel Buren and Hans Haacke in the 1960s and 1970s, or Andrea Fraser and Fred Wilson in the 1980s and 1990s – the contemporary activist art variant seeks to directly transform the material circumstances of the museum industry's internal operations, including the fate of those whose precarious 'dark matter' agency reproduces the logic of the art world itself. Equally notable is that in the fall of 2021, members of the Guggenheim's curatorial staff, employees who are normally considered management level, also petitioned to unionize alongside handlers, installers and so forth. Clearly something unprecedented is taking shape. And yet, there are some important semblances between today's unionization wave and the art activist critique of some 40 to 50 years ago worth noting.

In Chapters 3 and 5, I covered critical protest actions by 1960s groups such as Art Workers' Coalition, who initially sought a better work environment for living artists, virtually positioning themselves as laborers confronting management, before broadening their demands to include issues of racial justice, environmental action and an end to the US undeclared war in Southeast Asia. Similarly, today we find that organized pressure on museum directors to reform staff job precariousness has evolved into a critique of workplace culture and systemic racial and class biases. This includes audacious challenges by staff towards the innermost governance of certain museums themselves. Furthermore, this insider critique of the institution has also found its echo amongst external art activists.

RESTORATION JUSTICE

In 2018, over one hundred staff members at the Whitney Museum of American Art wrote an internal letter demanding that the position of one of the institution's highest-ranking board members, Warren Kanders, be terminated due to his ownership of Safariland, a company producing tear-gas canisters used against Latin American asylum seekers on the US border and Palestinian protesters in Gaza (see comments in Chapter 1).

After five months of weekly interventions staged in the museum's lobby by a coalition of groups organized by Decolonize This Place (DTP), Kanders finally stepped down.[4] The tipping point appears to have arrived when a group of eight diverse artists and the group Forensic Architecture simultaneously withdrew their work from the prestigious Whitney Biennial (notably, before the show even opened, one invited artist, Michael Rakowitz, had already refused to participate). In August 2019, artist Nan Goldin was among those arrested for protesting against art museum funding from the Sackler Trust, whose philanthropic wealth was made during the opioid pharmaceutical scandal.

Similar high art world shaming efforts led by Guerrilla Girls, Art Space Sanctuary and DTP, amongst other activist partners, were also employed to oust two MoMA Board members, Chairman Leon Black and Larry Fink. Protests over Black's personal ties to ultra-rich sex offender Jeffrey Epstein ultimately led to Black's resignation, although as of this writing, Fink, the founder and chairman of BlackRock, remains in place. On 10 October 2019, *Artforum* published a letter demanding Fink's resignation signed by over 200 arts professionals (myself included) that cites BlackRock's investments in 'prison companies, the war machine, and the destruction of the global environment'.[5] Meanwhile, the post-OWS groups Occupy Museums and Debtfair insist that Fink's corporation is the world's 'greatest single engine of debt extraction', adding that massive debt is the 'price of entry into the Art World'. The artist Michael Rakowitz demanded that a video of his included in an exhibition at MoMA PS1 be paused in protest, pithily saying, 'I kindly ask that MoMA please divest from Larry Fink and Leon Black as trustees so that I may un-pause my video and press play.'[6] The museum has yet to comply.

AESTHETICIZING POLITICS

If this sweeping critique were taking place only within the art world and solely carried out by activist artists who do not want to stop being artists, as Boris Groys proposes, the phenomenon would seem like less of a break with past forms of institutional critique. But it appears that we are witnessing a repetition that is also simultaneously contemporary and innovative. As if channeling Walter Benjamin's aphorism regarding high culture's hidden link with barbarism, art activism now seeks to uproot and reimagine not only this or that institutional practice, but the totality of high culture's deeper ideological structure, including its ties with centuries of colonial, patriarchal, heterosexual and class oppression. This critique also includes revoking a presumed institutional entitlement whereby Western museums display cultural treasures they appropriated, often illicitly, from colonized people.

In the fall of 2020, Emery Mwazulu Diyabanza, a Congolese activist, physically removed an African artifact from its exhibition perch at the Musée du Quai Branly in Paris (fig.13). Employees stopped him from exiting with the object, but not before Diyabanza tweeted the statement, 'I came here to take back what was stolen and plundered from us ... to take back what was pillaged from Africa.' The restitution activist and his comrades then similarly targeted several other European collections of African art in the following weeks. Ultimately fined as much as €5,000 for an identical intervention at the Louvre, Diyabanza has so far avoided incarceration for his restoration activism. In November 2020, France agreed to return some 27 African objects 'trapped' inside Europe's museums, repatriating them to Benin and Senegal, from which they were taken in colonial times. Diyabanza responded to the news, saying that 'this is a tiny fraction of what was taken ... it is African countries who should decide the timings of the restitution.'[7]

While Diyabanza does not claim to be an artist, nor am I proposing that he is one, his interventions, like so much activism today, do have all the hallmarks of a performance piece. Recognizing this congruity, as well as a shared set of decolonial objectives, members of the art coalition Strike MoMA cited the Congolese interventionist as an inspiration for their activism, stating that 'we are learning from each other, and reconnecting with legacies, promises, and lessons that came to a head in 1968, without apology'.[8] The allusion to the Situationists' total critique is right below the surface: a buried vanguard beach just beneath the concrete.

MONUMENTICIDE: ART WORLD JUSTICE AND BEYOND

In 2021, Strike MoMA, which is made up of members from Decolonise this Place (DTP), called for the complete rejection of what it described as the Museum's 'blood-soaked modernity', describing the institution itself as a 'messed up workplace [characterized by] elitism, hierarchy, inequality, precarity, disposability, anti-Blackness, misogyny.'[9] This statement points to a significant difference between the activists of the late 1960s and 1970s and those of today: the leading edge of the new wave of institutional critique is far less interested in reforming high culture than in calling for its abolition. As the group MTL (an arbitrary acronym devised in 2010 by socially engaged scholar Natasha Dhillon and Palestinian activist Amin Husain, who later, with other added members, morphed into GULF then DTP, and now Strike MoMA) put it in 2018, the principles of institutional critique are being 'pushed to a breaking point and opening onto something radically new and radically old at the same time ... The institution must be questioned in its very foundations.'[10] I will have more to say about the totalizing nature of this new critique of museums later on, but for now I want to focus on what appears to be a corollary surge of activism: the striking out against the public art manifestations of Western civilization and its narrative of colonialism and racial superiority; that is, the worldwide spectacle of monument takedowns, or monumenticides, that became particularly visible in the summer of 2020, but which had already begun years earlier with the anti-racist Rhodes (as in Cecil) Must Fall campaign in 2015, Cape Town, South Africa.

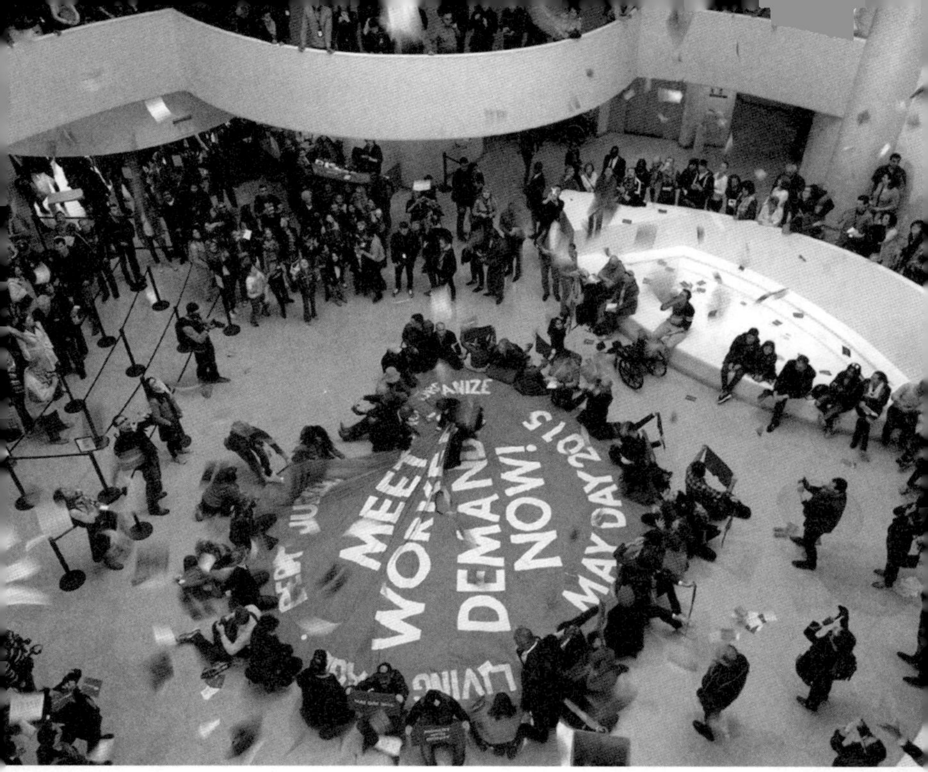

Fig.14 Global Ultra Luxury Faction (GULF) and Gulf Labor Coalition one-day occupation of the Guggenheim Museum, New York, 1 May 2015 to protest against inhuman working conditions for migrant laborers in Abu Dhabi where a new museum is under construction. Photo courtesy of Gulf Labor Coalition.

In 2016, a coalition of groups operating under the name Decolonial Cultural Front staged a protest over Brooklyn Museum's decision, ironically, to host a real estate development summit, while simultaneously exhibiting artifacts from recent art activist projects and occupations. Relaunching as Decolonize This Place (DTP), the alliance went on to produce a critical reinterpretation of New York's American Museum of Natural History, calling attention to its lingering white supremacist narrative of Manifest Destiny, which dates back to the institution's founding in the late 19th century.[11] Pressure from DTP and other activist groups, including Not An Alternative, soon focused on removing the racially offensive monument to President Theodore Roosevelt representing the former leader astride a massive stallion accompanied by two nameless guides walking below him, one African, the other Native American. The bronze tableau had been situated outside the building since 1940. The goal of its removal was only finally achieved in 2021, when the city announced that the monument would be relocated, a decision clearly compelled by the protest activism that followed the police murder of George Floyd (to be discussed in Chapter 13). Since Floyd's death, hundreds of racially offensive statues, monuments and memorials have been removed across the globe, some by government agencies, others by organized acts of direct protest vandalism.

POLITICAL PARADOXES OF THE TOTAL AESTHETIC/CULTURAL POLITICS

If it wasn't already clear during the heady years of tactical media's neo-Situationist techtopia, it has become unavoidably so today: activist art is no longer fixated upon or bound to a certain artistic precedent or aesthetic mandate, including the history of the avant-garde. Instead, artists who wish to become activists now draw freely, even promiscuously, upon the surplus content of the phantom archive and its previously dark mass of creative labor, accessible via the simplest of online search operations. This deep well of oppositional culture, both high and low, is available for repurposing and reactivation thanks to the accessibility of networked communications technology, as well as research by a new generation of artists, scholars and educators. Perhaps most consequently and paradoxically, though, the total aestheticization and generalization of a certain vanguard imagination by both cultural politics and capitalist society itself has helped open up access to this spectral archive – not only for pro-democratic and anti-racist activists, but also for those working in a precisely opposite mode of reactionary political agency, including global efforts to resuscitate fascism in a new, allegedly nationalist or patriotic guise, as I explore next.

Chapter 11

2016 and After: Winter Is Coming/Winter Is Here

> 'The immemorial intelligence displayed in the tricks and imitations of plants and fishes. From the depth of the ocean to the streets of modern megalopolises, there is a continuity and permanence in these tactics.'[1]
> *Michel de Certeau*

Many people will remember 2016 as the year that the US and UK began a sharp rightward turn against neoliberal globalism, a shift denoted by the contentious UK referendum on EU membership, leading to a turbulent British exit from the European Union, followed soon after by the election of a tax-evading, real estate speculator and TV entertainer as President of the United States. But in truth, these narrowly secured victories reflect the moment it became impossible to ignore the rising populist, reactionary opposition to both transnational neoliberalism and faltering, though still prevailing, liberal democratic policies providing safe haven for immigrants and refugees. As I write this, nearly 50 extreme conservative or ultra-right-wing populist parties hold some notable voting block above 10 per cent of governmental seats in much of Europe, including Scandinavia and the former Eastern Bloc nations.[2] They also have a growing influence in Australia, Japan, Peru and Indonesia, with far-right-tilting governments now seated in Hungary, Poland, Turkey, Afghanistan, the Gulf States, Israel, India, the Philippines and Brazil, and a substantial majority of extreme conservative legislators in the

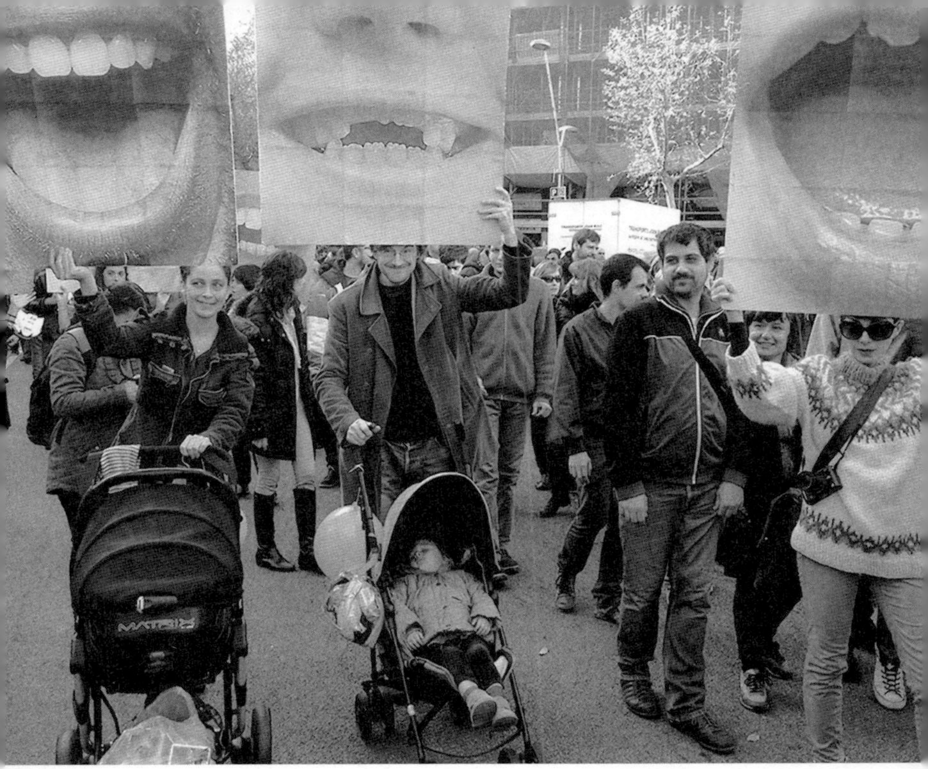

Fig.15 Thousands of people mobilized by the hashtag #SinMordaza gathered in the streets of Spanish cities in 2014 to protest a national 'gag law' making it a heavily finable offense to photograph or record police. Mounted photo enlargements of street art projects by Colectivo Enmedio.

United States. While these right-wing parties and movements take a variety of specific guises, they share a common ideology.

Perhaps the most outstanding feature of this ideology is support for strong nationalist governance over and above all other sectors of society. This means rolling back juridical independence to place courts under state and party control; the imposition of tariffs and other economic protectionist measures; instituting anti-immigration policies; placing limitations on freedoms of the press, speech, assembly, public protest, elections and the arts; as well as curtailing LGBTQ and women's rights. In some countries, such as Brazil, Hungary, Poland and the US, the right to abortion is either being rolled back, restricted or banned, while many of these far right parties explicitly align with anti-Islamic, and sometimes anti-Semitic, bigotry. It would not be an exaggeration to describe the situation as a return of authoritarian politics with a strong, increasingly explicit neo-fascist bent. Dismayingly, some adherents of this wave are also appropriating aspects of countercultural lifestyles, as well as Leftist protest tactics and online activism. Of course, significant differences linger just below the surfaces of these opposing agencies, returning us to one of the key threads of this book: the role of history and the phantom of resistance for the practice of the artist as activist. Nevertheless, the question of protest aesthetics must be raised with regard to populist-right actions, including the link between violence and art.

ALT-RIGHT AS FASHION CULTURE?

While 'Tea Party' anti-taxers have long mixed with both evangelical Christian conservatives and libertarian capitalists in the US – an alliance going back at least to the time of Ronald Reagan in the 1980s – they have gradually expanded their influence over other disaffected, white, working-class people. This change, or contagion if you will, has permitted overtly racist groups to organize far more openly in many parts of the US and elsewhere. In 2017, an appalling assembly of torch-wielding 'Unite the Right' marchers took over the streets of Charlottesville, Virginia, leading to the death of a counter-demonstrator, Heather Heyer, and violent attacks on other anti-fascist protesters, some of whom fought back. The situation reached a crescendo of sorts on 6 January 2021 when, stirred into action by a bitter, electorally defeated and soon to be ex-President, hundreds of populist right-wing demonstrators invaded the US Capitol building in Washington D.C. in search of 'traitors', with the intention of physically punishing those who they claimed had allegedly robbed them of their extreme nationalist candidate's victory. The significance of these anti-democratic forces loudly claiming to be the defenders of democracy, made within a prominent, symbolic seat of modern democracy, ensured that the world now came face-to-face with a long developing looking-glass reality, or what I call *the unpresent,* in which once familiar things turn abruptly otherworldly and strange, even if almost no one blinks, as further discussed in my conclusion.

Second-by-second video imagery of the unprecedented invasion of the Capitol reveals mostly white, mostly male attackers, very few of them wearing face masks openly denying the science behind protecting society against further spread of COVID-19. Some carried large Confederate, or Blue Lives Matter or Trump flags; others brandished trash-can-lid shields. One was notoriously dressed in a horn-and-fur-capped 'shaman' outfit and was covered in face paint while holding a US flag tipped with an arrowhead, even though he is not Indigenous. The performative spectacle of pro-Trump mayhem was immediately distributed by mainstream media. Billions of viewers witnessed it. The chaotic swells of enraged bruisers, some determined to appear as paramilitary commandos, was accompanied by larger swarms of intruders who repeatedly mumbled mantras about a 'stolen election' or stupefyingly shouted that they couldn't believe what they were doing was even real. Indeed, at times it felt like we viewers were watching a live-action role-playing game (LARP) unfold. Although, assuredly, 6 January 2021 was a contemporary form of aesthetic protest with its own (distorted) utopian-populist dimension.[3] Unlike the Arab Spring, Occupy Wall Street or BLM protest actions, however, it was not prefigurative of a better future to come, but an expression of desire to return to an imagined past that never existed. And rather than celebrating dissimilarity, unconventionality and heterogeneity, as most of the contemporary activist Left does, members of the attempted Capitol Hill coup and other ultra-patriotic groups dream of a populist right-wing fantasy rooted in near-religious adoration of national, folkloric and racial identities that previously guaranteed social privileges for a limited sector of the population – a phenomenon consistent with the neo-authoritarian shift we are witnessing around the globe.

Significantly, along with the resurgence of the Ku Klux Klan and other white nationalist and neo-Nazi groups with older memberships, there is a new, younger and less familiar variant of racist authoritarianism emerging today, gathered under the heading of the alt-right. It includes groups such as the Proud Boys, Oath Keepers, Fraternal Order of the Alt-Knights, Boogaloo, Revolt Through Tradition, and Patriot Front, whose members have carried out masked, violent attacks on Black Lives Matter and Antifa, as well as immigrants and queer people in the streets of Ferguson, Charlottesville, San Antonio, Portland, New York and Los Angeles. Notably, some also aim to be cultural trendsetters, donning pleated yellow kilts or adopting the look of 1970s British skinheads wearing designer clothes, rather than Confederate hats, Nazi uniforms or even dark blue two-piece suits.

Fully conversant with cyber-networking technologies, these new alt-right groups repurpose methods first developed by tactical media activists over two decades earlier, including culture jamming, the impersonation of adversaries and forms of *détournemen*t, although they are unlikely to have directly studied Situationism. They have even constructed a parallel Internet for their misogynist memes and patriarchal trolling. But unlike the Situationist critique of the 1960s, with its total war against an all-encompassing bureaucratic state and its media spectacle, the target of today's ultra-Right is the debilitated democracies of neoliberal, post-Brexit republics. In sum, we are confronted with the possibility that De Certeau's everyday resistor who deploys 'clever tricks' and a 'hunter's cunning', is mutating into something unforeseen and unnamable; a viral, resentment-filled xenophobe bent on breaking down the compromised collective defense systems of socially fatigued and crisis-plagued centrist democracies.[4]

PUSHING BACK

Activists and artists in Europe have had a longer time to develop a set of responses to this grim situation. The UK-based Extinction Rebellion (XR) movement, for example, began with a focus on environmental activism and has, since the 2020 Black Lives Matter protests, evolved to encompass other issues including a decolonial critique. In August 2021, the group staged a performance in front of the London Stock Exchange on Paternoster Square where performative demonstrators garbed in flame-colored rags, masks and headgear bathed themselves in faux human blood all the while denouncing the tainted colonialist money undergirding the British economy. The protest was the largest mobilization by the massively networked organization to date, bringing the city to 'a standstill for days at a time,' writes artist and filmmaker Oliver Ressler, as XR blockaded bridges and streets, ultimately forcing the UK parliament to declare a 'climate emergency'.[5] Ressler, who has produced extensive video works about XR, reflects on contemporary art activism's evolving alliance with non-art activists, noting that:

> artists' involvement in these movements has developed significantly over the last few years. Not so long ago, artists mainly contributed to the movements' visual identity, creating banners, posters, websites, and so on. Today, however, artists and cultural producers increasingly tend to become central protagonists, whether as spokespeople or in shaping media tactics and broader strategy.[6]

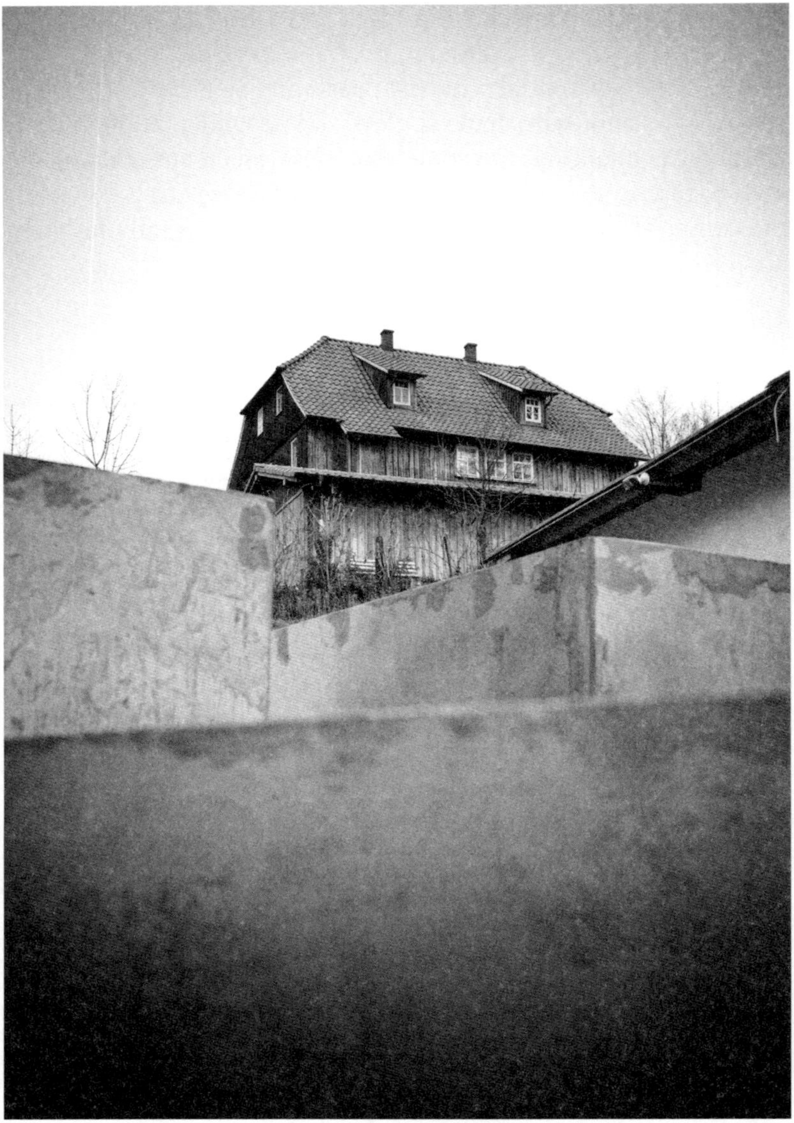

Fig.16 Center for Political Beauty's scale replica reconstruction of the Memorial to the Murdered Jews of Europe, across the street from ultra-nationalist parliamentary member Björn Höcke's home in Bornhagen, Germany, 2017.

Ressler's important observation signals a crucial theme that underscores this book; that the art of activism and the activism of art no longer simply intersect, instead, they increasingly double one another, like a Venn Diagram flipped and reflected back as if in a looking glass.

Elsewhere, in Serbia, where nationalist, religious and neo-fascist forces have converged in pursuit of political dominance within a post-socialist, neoliberal framework, art activists have engaged in a double critique that rejects privatized corporate culture and the 'ethnification' of the country by a reactionary government. When the newly constructed Museum of Contemporary Art in Belgrade (MSUB) reopened in the fall of 2017, its curatorial policy was 'entirely in line with the ministry's new right-wing cultural strategy', the Serbian artist Rena Rädle explains, including promoting exhibitions pivoting around folklore and myths supporting a fabled Serbian national identity.[7] Protests ensued. Arrests followed. One group of artists calling themselves 'The Unbribables' distributed images of sandwiches in front of the MSUB to symbolize corrupt election bribing, while wearing masks printed with the face of Serbian President Aleksandar Vučić. The museum called the police, and when Unbribable activist Vladan Jeremić tried to enter the building, he was taken into custody. The MSUB's director later stated, in language reminiscent of Hans Haacke's 1971 Guggenheim censorship event (see Chapter 6), that these types of artistic expression 'exceed certain limits of civilized norms'.[8]

Such treatment is not reserved for artists, Rädle adds; it is also being directed against 'journalists or any sort of "whistleblowers"'.[8] Relatedly, Spain's 2015 Organic Law for the Protection of Public Security is known colloquially as the 'gag law' because it levels fines of €600–30,000 for taking a photo of or otherwise recording police officers, engaging in non-violent resistance to authority, attempting to prevent an eviction, or occupying a bank lobby. In response, the group Colectivo Enmedio produced oversized images of human mouths shouting, talking and smiling, and carried them into the streets (fig.15). Its members described the actions as #SinMordaza

(Without Mordaza, the name of the law in question), insisting 'we could not keep our mouths closed'.[10] In Greece, despite the electoral and legislative defeat of the far right Golden Dawn party, incidents of racist and extreme nationalist violence against immigrants and Leftists are the highest in Europe, according to a report from the University of Oslo. Artists have reacted with street art and sustainable mockstitutional squatted spaces that 'perform' an aesthetics of autonomous community politics. But on 19 May 2021 perhaps the best known of these informal centers, the Occupied Theater EMPROS, was raided by Athens police and shuttered after a decade of activity.[11]

Ever since coming into power in 2015, Poland's far right Law and Justice Party has faced weekly opposition from women and supporters who gather to protest against strict anti-abortion legislation in ever-growing marches known as 'Black Mondays'. The events have also become increasingly visual – one could say, aestheticized – like many similar protest actions in recent years. Hand-drawn caricatures of conservative government leaders are carried aloft, and picket signs feature puns and witty slogans. One protester – perhaps an artist, perhaps not – fabricated a glowing coffin-shaped womb that she wore over her belly, with the label, 'I won't be a living coffin', to demonstrate opposition to new right-wing Polish laws that will force people to carry a fetus even if it is terminally ill or physically damaged. Another protest icon is a bright red lightning bolt designed by Ola Jasionowska, a member of the Consortium for Postartistic Practices; it is often accompanied by the slogan 'Be careful, we warn you!' directed at male, anti-choice authorities.[12]

One activist art group focused on directly confronting the populist far right's support structure is the Center for Political Beauty (CPB) in Germany. It has prioritized creative tactics aimed not only at confronting and critiquing but also defunding ultranationalist groups, including the Alternative für Deutschland (AfD), which in 2017 gained close to one hundred elected seats in the German Bundestag. Declaring itself an artistic 'assault troop that establishes moral beauty, political poetry, and human magnanimity', the CPB claims that it 'fuses the power of fantasy with the power of history'.[13] Ultra nationalists describe the CPB quite differently, going so far as to claim that it is not making art, but rather engaged in terrorism.[14] One CPB project involved fabricating a miniature version of Berlin's Memorial to the Murdered Jews of Europe and installing it right outside the home of AfD member Björn Höcke, who once proclaimed that the actual memorial testifies to the fact that Germans are 'the only people in the world to plant a monument of shame in the heart of their capital'.[15] CPB countered by saying that Germany should not only learn from its history but also take action: 'Resistance is an art that must hurt, irritate, and unsettle.'[16]

There's no doubt that a link exists between violence, even brutality, and aesthetics – the history of the avant-garde is swarming with symbolic and at times real connections between the two, including Filippo Tommaso Marinetti's adoration of mechanical warfare, André Breton's Surrealist fantasy of firing a pistol blindly into a crowd and Antonin Artaud's Theatre of Cruelty. Indeed, scholar Bernadette Buckley tells us that the imagination constitutes another order of reality and that it is 'the *imaginative* power of terror which gives it its force – the imagining of what *might* take place'.[17] But we can also dissect this association in a different way, by contrasting, for example, CPB's activist art project with the incendiary works of Santiago Sierra, who recently turned a former German synagogue into a gas chamber filled with carbon monoxide, making it viewable only with a gas mask, or the Swedish artist Dan Park's placement of boxes labeled 'Zyklon B' – the Nazi's extermination gas – before a Jewish community center in Malmö, Sweden.

While Sierra insists his actions were a vanguardist attempt to challenge liberal complacency, Park's alignment with far right interests likely contributed to his imprisonment on charges of inciting racial agitation and defamation. Notably, however, both Sierra and Park aestheticize traumatic memories in order to call out what they see as the hypocritical liberalism of the art world and mainstream media. Sierra's work, once so startling only a decade ago, appears today as abstract and indefinite; meanwhile, the implosion of liberal democracy, perhaps the artist's favorite target, is no doubt at the crux of this critical deflation , as is the rise of the far right. By contrast, CPB specifically targets the ideological and financial foundations of those who disseminate hate speech, thus politicizing contemporary art through the archival agency of memory, rather than aestheticizing the memory of trauma.

REPURPOSING THE SURPLUS ARCHIVE OF ACTIVIST ART

The populist Right typically reduces complex political situations to scenarios of 'us versus them', but it also tends to betray a second-rate, Hollywood-like imagination glued fast to an immobilized past stocked with paper-thin versions of nationalist warriors, Confederate rebels and blond, swastika-ornamented storm troopers. By contrast, movements such as BLM, OWS or 15-M/Los Indignados in Spain, 2011, celebrate a critically interpreted and repurposed pluralism that draws inventively, rather than rigidly, from the surplus archive of dark matter resistance against unfreedom. It is the essential uncertainty of this archive from below that leads the progressively minded activist artist to a politics of critical memory, as opposed to the populist Right's servile memory of historical submissiveness, which posits obedience to the false essentialist powers of patriarchy, colonialism and racial supremacy. And when not overtly mimicking an inglorious past, right-wing populists turn to direct violence and pageantries of terror based on those same mythical origin stories, as witnessed in Charlottesville in 2017 and Washington, D.C. in early 2021.

That stated, culture does not lead historical change in and by itself. No matter how inspirational, imaginative or prefigurative in ambition or in scope. Activist art cannot simply vault over the material and historical conditions of a given moment or location. What follows next, therefore, is a set of sobering thumbnail sketches in which artistic activism has played a central resistant role against authoritarianism, and yet the outcomes, at least to date, are a setback or defeat of progressive social change. One prominent feature that links these examples together is the apparent fluidity of role switching between 'professional' artists and everyday individuals who become swept up in an aesthetics of resistance towards repressive regimes. And here, despite my criticisms, we also discover a politically positive role played by the emergence of cultural politics as discussed ahead.

ACTIVISM ALSO FAILS

Failure is admittedly a bit of an overstatement here, for even when resistance to oppressive circumstances is reversed – as the brief inventory below demonstrates – activism will continue by other means; and in contemporary times, this typically means moving into cyberspace via social networks, including encrypted platforms. Therefore, perhaps the post-1968 'long march' now winds its way not through offices, schools and factories, but through the digital ether? At least until conditions permit otherwise?

Syria

Street artist Abu Malik al-Shami, aka 'Syria's Banksy', has created sardonic activist murals starting in 2019, the eighth year of revolutionary resistance to Bashar al-Assad's dictatorial regime, in public works that for example combine Van Gogh's *Starry Night* with a government helicopter bombing terrorized children. Notably, the anti-Assad uprising began as popular outrage after authorities tortured 15 tenth-grade boys for spray-painting anti-government graffiti in the city of Daraa. The artist is now living in Turkey after many years in Idlib.

Afghanistan

In Kabul, street artists Shamsia Hassani, Kabul Knights and Malina Suliman, collectively known as the ArtLords, painted ebullient graffiti and murals in Kabul, often depicting

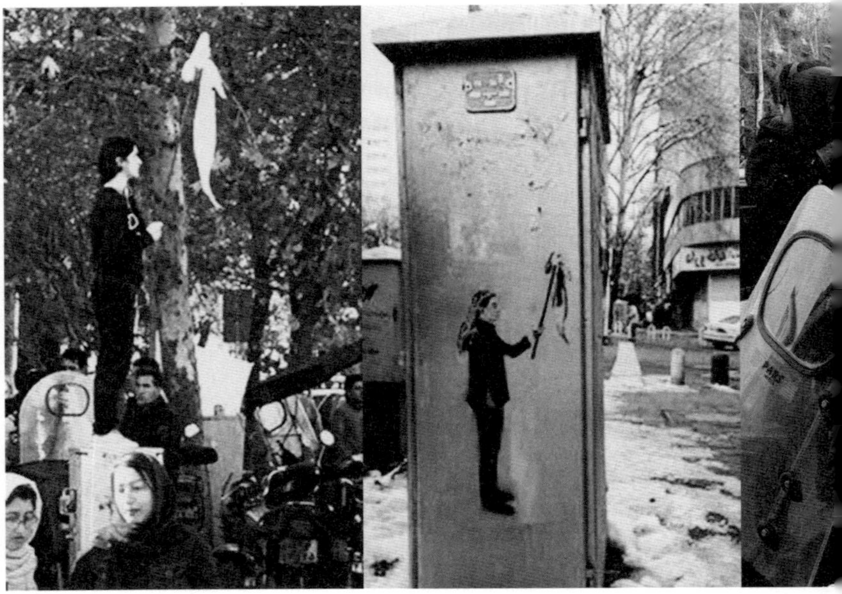

Fig.17 *The Geometry of Resistance*, Revolution Street, Tehran, Iran. Before being arrested in December 2018, Vida Movahed stood defiantly on a telecommunications utility box, waving her headscarf like a flag to protest against compulsory hijab laws. Other women began to repeat the act. In response, the government welded a peaked structure to the top of the utility box. An anonymous individual then circulated plans for producing a DIY device to circumvent the structure, permitting protestors to stand again in defiance. Image composite from online sources, @gsholette.

celebratory images of women and children, but especially girls laughing, studying and playing music – activities repressed under former Taliban rule. On 15 August 2021, when US and allied forces left in the face of the Taliban's return, ArtLords tweeted that their stubborn pursuit of street art was akin to musicians performing on a sinking *Titanic*. As of this writing, Afghan street artists have gone into exile, their murals whitewashed.

Gaza

Remarkably resilient, Palestinian activists in 2018 Gaza constructed an elaborate 'Great Right of Return' tent village outside

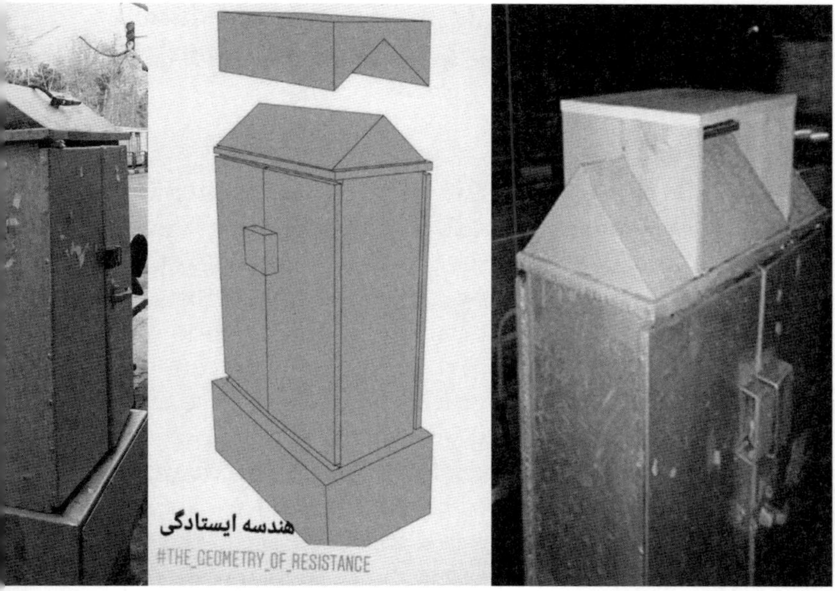

the perimeter fence of land forbidden to their own community. At this base camp of resistance, they generated a social infrastructure with university seminars, free drawing classes, communal meals, medical clinics and tactical media projects, including flying kites and helium-filled balloons with counter-propaganda letters attached over the border to members of the Israeli Defense Forces.[18] Nonetheless, as Human Rights Watch reports, systematic discrimination of Palestinians has devastated their economy and wellbeing for Gaza's 5 million inhabitants.

Hong Kong

Members of the Lausan Collective observe that Hong Kong protesters from 2019 to 2020 involved everyday people who 'fell out of their daily schedules [and] created art'.[19] Thus, these protest aesthetics were not limited to professionals, but incorporated a multitude of resistant forms ranging from graffiti, chalk drawings and graphics to Post-it Notes and photographs, demanding independence from mainland

China (PRC). Distressingly, the Lausan group self-dissolved in the autumn of 2021, during the crackdown on protests by HK authorities aligned with the PRC.

Belarus

In Europe's former socialist East, Belarus has recently witnessed mass resistance to more than 20 years of President Alexander Lukashenko's authoritarianism and election rigging. One particular wall on Chervyakova Street in Minsk witnessed a recurring street-art battle between protesters – who were not necessarily artists – painting portraits of two banned, anti-government DJs. State officials buffed out these forbidden figures, who soon reappeared, were again covered over with patches of beige paint, before returning again overnight, in an image-based melee that lasted months. The once anonymous space surrounding the wall was secretly renamed 'The Square of Changes' (Площадь Перемен). Since then, most Belarusian informal and professional protest artists have either since ceased acting or been arrested, although resistance continues online with networks of 'Cyber-partisan' hacktivists (and regarding wartime Ukraine, see my conclusions in Chapter 13).

Cuba

Known for her physically daring performances, former Havana-based artist Tania Bruguera pushed her practice so close to direct social intervention that Cuban authorities label her a dissident, not artist. Now relocated to the US, Bruguera's concept of 'artivism' and Arte Útil argues that art should function directly 'with/in reality', insisting that 'failure is not a possibility.'[20] Still active on the island, in 2018 artist Luis Manuel Otero Alcántara circulated a covert photo of himself holding a four-foot-long sledgehammer aloft, poised to strike the storefront of Havana's Giorgio G. VIP retail outlet, chock-full of fashionable commodities selling for hundreds more than the salary of average Cubans.[21] The smash-and-grab *tableau vivant* mimics classic Socialist Realist art, seemingly asking: whither socialist equality in today's Cuba? Perhaps tellingly, the static photographic image is flash-frozen in time. Alcántara has been arrested and detained numerous times.

Egypt, Iran and Turkey

Following Egypt's 2011 Tahrir Square revolution, street art muralists were targeted for arrest, as their work on Mohammed Mahmoud Street was whitewashed. In Iran, the women of Enghelab-e Islami Street (Revolution Street) defiantly fought for their freedom, performatively attaching headscarves to thin sticks and waving these as a protest against compulsory hijab laws, resulting in arrests (fig.17). In Turkey, the remarkable Gezi Park protests of 2013 birthed a new type of activism involving standing still in public. These silent, immobile performances forced Turkish authorities to either arrest those doing absolutely nothing, or allow an obvious act of dissent to proceed and inspire others.

Of course, to suggest that artistic repression and censorship is exclusive to non-Western or non-liberal nations is to ignore the growing challenge that artists face in self-proclaimed democratic states, such as Spain's previously discussed 'gag law', and recent UK legislation that could make public demonstrations by Extinction Rebellion, among others, illegal because of noise and disruption to the flow of urban movement and commerce. But, if cold reality shows that resistance also works in reverse, generating an intensification of oppression, this has seldom prevented an aesthetics of resistance from endeavoring to challenge subjugation. Is it possible, therefore, that thanks to art's historical social autonomy, and the rise of a cultural politics and tactical activism that is detached from traditional vanguard ideologies, unionism and party politics (as previously discussed), contemporary art activism summons a seemingly unquenchable force for social justice, which explains its expanding durability today? As discussed in the next chapter, whatever limitations this paradigm may present, no contemporary social movement better exemplifies the art of activism's current robustness than Black Lives Matter.

Chapter 12

Black Lives Matter: Fugitivity in Plain Sight

> 'It's an aesthetic thing; blackness is an affront to the persistence of whiteness. It's the reason that so little has been done to stop genocide in Africa. This invisibility – this erasure out of the complex history of our life and time – is the greatest source of my longing.'[1]
> *Carrie Mae Weems*

> 'Black Lives Matter reinvented our activist vocabulary by producing a subversive symbolic order that puts together code and flow, information and reaction, surplus and collective imagination ... showing its codependence with physical, collective acts of appearance and affirmation.'[2]
> *Carlos Garrido Castellano*

Eight photographic enlargements mounted on portable panels are carried through New York City streets to form a pair of penetrating, enormous eyes. The year was 2014, and the mobile art project led a column of tens of thousands of marchers who convened around the hashtag #BlackLivesMatter (BLM). The Paris-based, street artist JR created the work by digitally magnifying the gaze of Eric Garner, an unarmed Black man killed by a police officer who had put him in a chokehold on Staten Island earlier that year. JR increased the images of Garner's eyes and brow over a hundred times to generate a moving memorial that stared out at the living from a place of unjustified disappearance and loss (fig.18). In another part

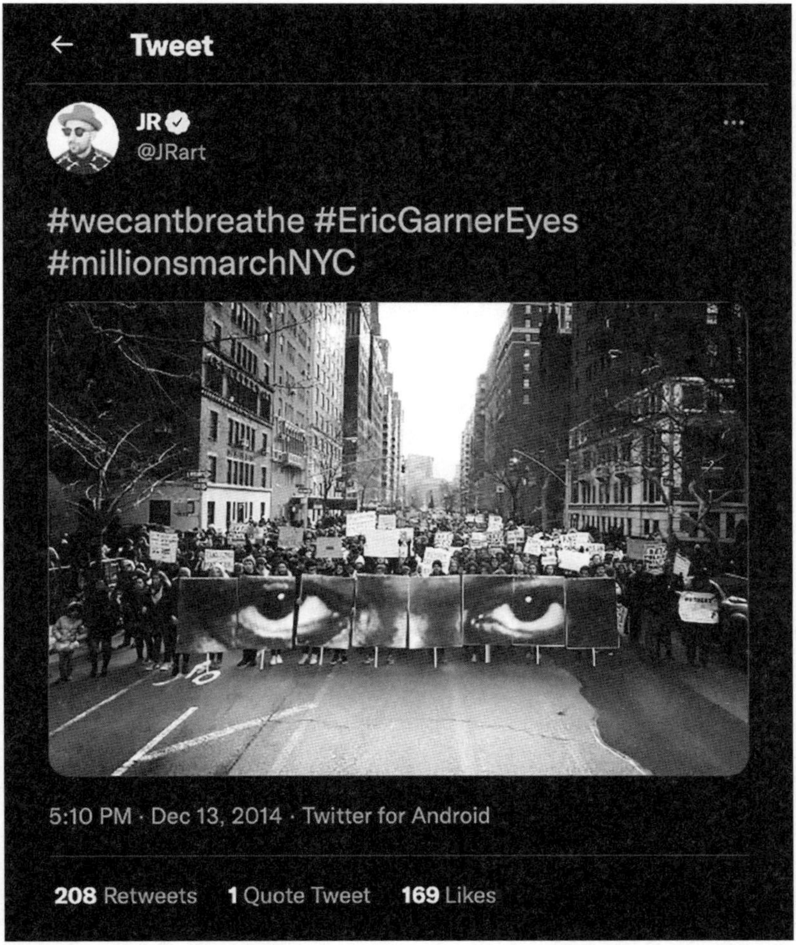

Fig.18 Artist JR's mobile demonstration piece based on Eric Garner's eyes during the 2014 Millions March NYC for all those innocent people of colour killed by the misuse of police force, https://twitter.com/jrart/status/543890644184629248?lang=en.

of the march, bright red floating letters broadcast a simple demand: 'This Stops Today.' Elsewhere, cardboard cut-out hands were raised in a 'don't shoot' gesture, as flash mobs, dance performances and an enormous papier-mâché puppet of Michael Brown – a Black youth who was shot six times by police in Ferguson, Missouri – combined protest with the exultation of temporarily 'owning' the streets, effectively politicizing and repurposing community trauma as an aesthetic event.

If visual art activism can precipitate and amplify a broader rupture with the status quo, the BLM associated public interventions proved this is still possible. In Ferguson itself, artist Damon Davis wheat-pasted meter-high #allhandsondeck posters on to boarded-up storefronts along West Florissant Avenue, the street where Brown was shot by police (fig.19). Davis's project took place during the wait for the grand jury's decision on the killing. Ultimately, no charges were filed against the white officer. Around the same time, in Washington D.C., artist Omolara Williams McCallister 'culture-jacked' the city's Christmas display, placing over a thousand handmade, BLM-stenciled ornaments in public spaces. And in Salt Lake City, Utah, a pair of palms-up, monumental bronze hands entitled 'Serve and Protect' were spattered with thick crimson paint, temporarily repurposing the publicly commissioned sculpture installed outside the local Public Safety Building into a testament of dissent.

These street actions also carried over into a torrent of sharable web content that repeated and amplified the BLM project, which in turn has had a widespread impact on the high cultural establishment, compelling changes in institutional policies and museum hiring practices, as well as an unmistakable broadening of who gets to pass through the art world gates. Little wonder, therefore, that BLM was ranked the top art world influencer in *ArtReview*'s 'Power 100' for 2020, as mentioned at the start of this book (fig.1). Regardless of the difficulties involved in self-organizing and group governance – impediments that increasingly plague BLM but have always come with the terrain of activist leadership – the movement has unquestionably forced a palpable change within the dynamics of art activism going forwards, and in a certain sense, also looking back.

The dam really broke, however, with the 2020 murder of George Floyd, an unarmed Black man who was handcuffed and suffocated by a white Minnesota police officer. Documented on cell-phones, circulated on the Internet and viewed a billion times in two weeks, Floyd's grisly, 9-minute-and-29-second public murder touched off a worldwide monumenticide movement demanding – and in many instances carrying out by fiat – the removal of statues and memorials that directly or indirectly support white supremacy. Despite the COVID-19 pandemic lockdown, which quarantined most nonessential workers in their homes, a wave of monument takedowns, both official and unofficial, some carried out at night despite armed guards protecting certain statutes, grabbed hold of the world's collective attention throughout the summer of 2020. One of the most dramatic of these monumenticide moments was the toppling of a statue depicting slave trader Edward Colston in Bristol, England, which was not only dragged off its pedestal, but the bronze monument wound up at the bottom of the River Avon, whose port once led the nation in transporting a half million slaves between 1730 and 1745.

While acts of protest vandalism date back at least to Gustave Courbet's role in the destruction of the Vendôme Column during the Paris Commune of 1871, returning often, for example after independence in the 1960s throughout the region of the Caribbean, the combination of criticism, fury and festivity found in recent monument takedowns – including colorful graffiti defacements that linger as a type of site-specific critique and the construction of temporary, public counter-memorials – reflects a far-reaching rejection of non-egalitarian politics, white supremacy and other aspects of patriarchal, heterocentric culture. The reactivation of past forms of aesthetic protest, and the withdrawal of cultural practices from society, is joined therefore by a new call for abolition as three alternating directions for activist art in the present moment. More on this to come.

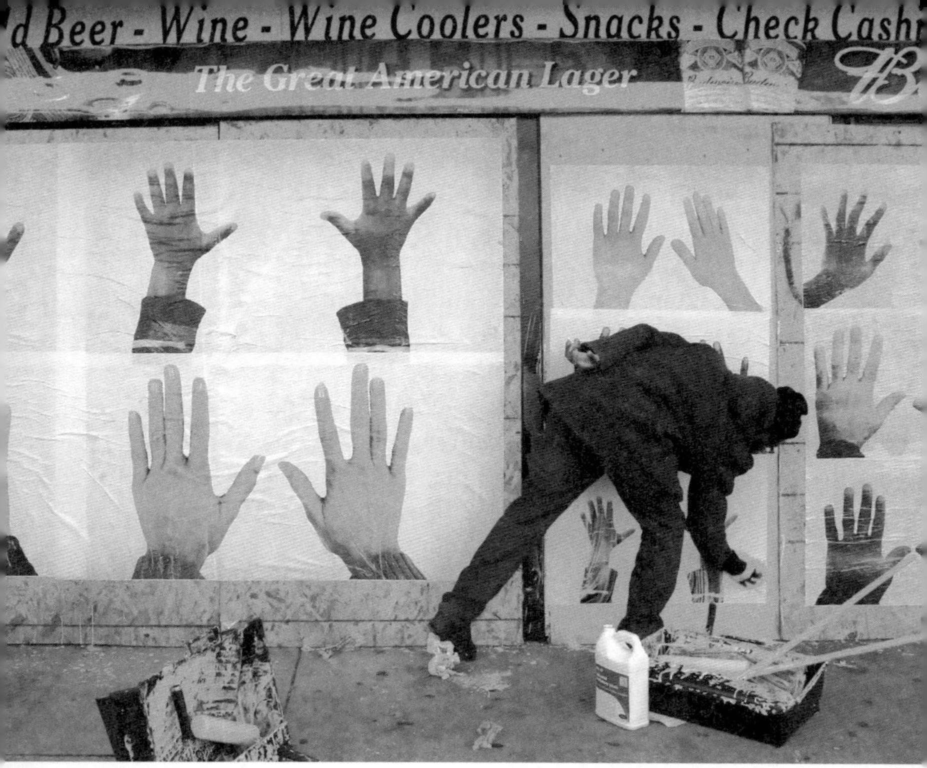

Fig.19 Damon Davis in 2015, wheat-pasting his #allhandsondeck street poster project as Ferguson, Missouri, awaited the grand jury decision on the police killing of Michael Brown on 19 November 2014. Ultimately, no charges were filed against officer Darren Wilson.

'To appear is to matter', writes Nicholas Mirzoeff, reinterpreting Jacques Rancière's assertion that gaining visibility generates a politics of appearance – a struggle within a long history of the white establishment seeing Black bodies and representations of African Americans and other people of color as foremost a matter of visual and physical control.[3] By claiming ownership of this negation, and turning it into a sometimes solemn, sometimes celebratory display of public non-compliance, BLM-inspired street actions do exactly the opposite. The movement's protest aesthetic explicitly refuses to acknowledge the centuries-old optics of a disciplinary society that depends upon the orderly maintenance of non-white peoples, enforced through the policing of images and physical presence. And once fully visible, Blackness is impossible to re-conceal; it redefines visuality itself. Aided by cell phone cameras, citizen journalism and online distribution, 'low-resolution photographs and videos that captured the particular set of appearances that can be called Black Lives Matter have become a genre, a symptom of how American culture is now', Mirzoeff affirms.[4]

It's not that Blackness had never previously interjected itself into white high culture. Such interventions happened on many occasions, including the Afro-Surrealist movement of Aimé and Suzanne Césaire and René Ménil in the 1940s, Emory Douglas and the Black Panther Party in the 1960s and 1970s, as well as the Black Arts Movement, about which Amiri Baraka wrote, 'our feeling of us-ness is the beginning of our redefinition of ourselves as us-in-the-world'.[5] The BLM project not only picks up these archival threads and reactivates them in the present, but also places political emphasis on Blackness as the irrefutable materiality of interruption, both within and apart from mainstream culture. Or, as Fred Moten puts it, rather than accepting not being white as a pathological state in relation to the ruling order, Black political resistance refuses to serve as 'an other', embracing instead a certain homelessness and lived 'ontology of disorder' that makes possible 'an openness disruptive of the very idea of set – of accumulative and unaccumulable differences, differings, departures without origin, leavings that continually defy the natal occasion in general even as they constantly bespeak the previous'.[6] The contemporary activist complement to this *fugitive state of being in the world* is to foreground a certain resistant 'undercommons' (Moten's term) that remains in plain sight of everyday life. Its oppositionality takes the form of confronting police, state authorities and the media, all within clear sight of the white establishment, and is distributed via social networks as well as within the haughty realm of the fine art establishment.

What's more, while BLM has unquestionably set a new high bar for protest aesthetics, the movement has also raised practical and theoretical challenges for the artist who would be activist, further beclouding the line between art and activism, artist and activist. The movement provides further evidence that this is precisely a contested space: theoretically, practically, literally. After the shooting of Michael Brown, writes St Louis-based art educator Sarah Hermes Griesbach, 'artists have been at the center of this movement', quickly and significantly adding that this includes 'artists who never considered themselves as such'.[7] Which is to say that from an artistic perspective, the protest aesthetic of BLM concretizes one major theme of this study: the inversion and mutual causality between art activism and activism.

The Contemporary Artist as Activist: Conjectures, Hauntologies and Inconclusions

'History only exists if there is a tomorrow.'[1]
Hito Steyerl

'Rather than only thinking about the aesthetic qualities of space, artists can aim to topple the neoliberal scaffold that holds capitalism steady above us, like a firmament.'[2]
Shellyne Rodriguez

'There isn't a positive interpretive discourse in art for activist engagement. Because even to call something activist engagement is to give it a kind of functionalist cast.'[3]
Coco Fusco

'Activist art functions as a glitch within art history that threatens to invert the "figure and ground" of the narrative.'[4]
Kim Charnley

With apologies to philosopher Giorgio Agamben, it seems that we have entered an era of bare art: a condition in which high culture is stripped of its claims to freedom and autonomy as virtually everything about 'art' as it has long been defined is peeling away, leaving a raw, exposed and vulnerable thing behind.[5] The economic and political contradictions of the art

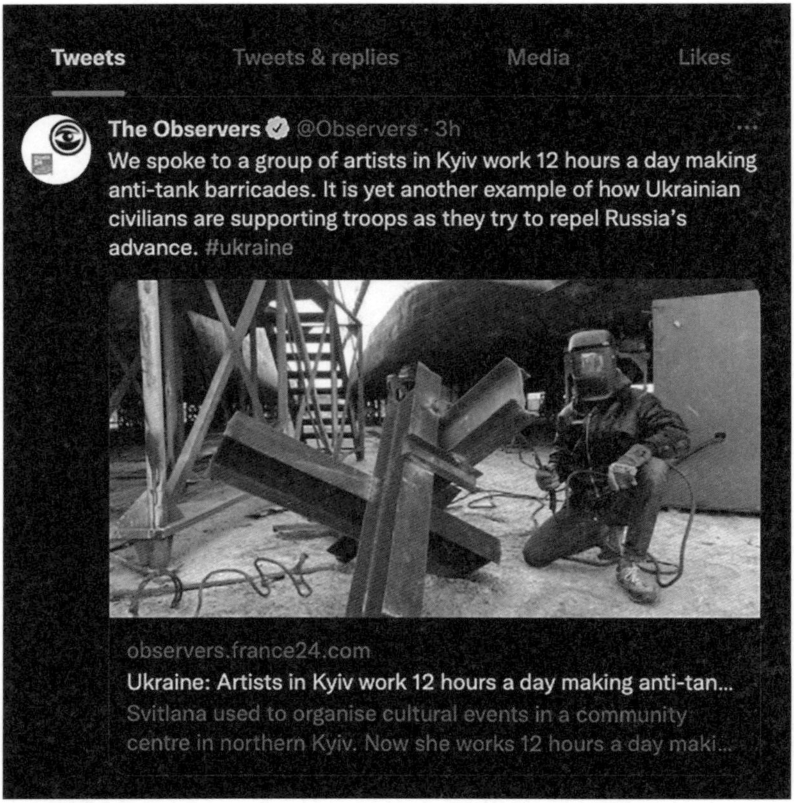

Fig.20 Tweeted photograph from 6 March 2022, less than two weeks after the direct Russian invasion of Western Ukraine.

world have become impossible to conceal, much as the financialization of everyday life has become resoundingly evident within all levels of existence.[6] High culture's internal aesthetic character is now manifest as so many flagrant and utterly ordinary attributes, so many data points, flippable abstract paintings and skyrocketing NFTs (digital Non-Fungible Tokens). Meanwhile, the desire by 1960s Conceptual and political artists to transform their elite social position into that of 'cultural workers' appears at last to have been fulfilled as artists appear today as just another innovative worker, no more, no less, *or almost so.* For one does not have to disagree with Dave Beech when he convincingly argues that artistic labor is not commodified wage labor in order to recognize that virtually everything else about art is marketized, monetized and reified.[7] As an over-educated and redundant labor force, cultural workers appear to be part of the Professional Managerial Class (PMC), and a painfully all too visible faction of the cognitariat, or creative labor force. But this positioning does not preclude the possibility of resistance, as we have seen, and as we will undoubtedly continue to witness.[8] Only the understanding of this artistic oppositionality requires new insights and analysis going forwards.

The inverse and directly related phenomenon of bare art is an unconditional aestheticization of everyday life in which the Situationists' dreaded mass spectacle has expanded to epic proportions. When life becomes an unending visual pageant of commodities, news, memes and brands, both on- and offline, the horizon of resistance is itself radically altered, although not evaporated. A shifted terrain calls for updated tactics, new strategies and archival recoveries as well as an exacting precision with regard to one's opponents, as we saw with the Center for Political Beauty in Chapter 11, or with Laurie Jo Reynold's Tamms Year Ten 'legislative art' campaign that successfully helped shut down a notorious maximum security prison known for its inhuman solitary confinement practices. In this way, the legacy of progressive art activism – if I can be so bold – detaches itself from the fabulist concoctions of the ultra-Right and other forces of authoritarian oppression, as they don the appearance of order and virtue, in order to assure White minority rule and other forms of historically retrenched absolutism. Let us look more closely at this new topography.

PROTEST AESTHETICS

Collective bodies choreographed in exquisite public movements, bold graphic protest imagery, exclamatory texts, electrified social spaces and aural sound eruptions – the power of such dissident aesthetics unfolding within a highly spectacularized society has not escaped notice by intellectuals, theorists and academics. In just over the past decade, an accelerating series of essays, books and conferences have focused on the aesthetic dimensions of political expression. What is unusual about this scholarship is that it approaches these sensory forms of resistance as artistic practice, without reservation or the need to explain some elusive difference between art and activism. The authors also come from a wide range of fields: not surprisingly, art theory and cultural studies, but also anthropology, urbanism, gender, postcolonial, globalization and immigration studies, as well as political science.

A sampling of these treatises includes Julia Ramírez-Blanco's *Artistic Utopias of Revolt*; Yates McKee's *Strike Art*; Nato Thompson's *Living as Form* and *Seeing Power*; Peter Weibel's *Global Activism*; Aiden McGarry, Itir Erhart et al.'s *The Aesthetics of Global Protest*; Pnina Werbner et al.'s *The Political Aesthetics of Global Protest,* Katarzyna Marciniak and Imogen Tyler's *Immigrant Protest*; Stephanie Hartle and Darcy White's *Art, Protest and Resistance in an Uncertain World*; Martin Patrick's *Across the Art/Life Divide*; Kim Charnley's *Sociopolitical Aesthetics*; Mirzoeff and Pope's *The Appearance of Black Lives Matter*; and preceding all these studies, the aptly named *The Journal of Aesthetics & Protest,* which has been in print and online since 2001. At the risk of abbreviating many complex arguments and much diligent research, a consensus appears to have formed around the idea that aesthetics is not only 'harnessed by sociopolitical and sociocultural actors,' as the authors of *The Aesthetics of Global Protest* assert (not in itself an especially new or provocative idea), but that by engaging in protest actions aesthetically, oppositional movements acquire 'the power to transform existing structures, ideas, and orthodoxies'.[9] I am reminded of the lofty expectations for art's radically transfigurative social capacity, as set forth by Saint-Simon back in the early 19th century and touched upon in Chapter 1. Only this injunction is fulfilled today not in a collaborative triumvirate with scientists and industrialists, but rather in contrast or outright opposition to them.

Still, exactly how and when did the artistic dream of historical agency, as laid out by Martha Rosler at the start of this volume, become so potent and real in the present, and why has it apparently breached the confines of art to enter the everyday world? For few would deny the robust growth of an 'art of protest' in recent years, one whose material dimensions are manifest in its 'visual dimensions, its silence, its vocalization, and its rhythm', as described by McGarry et al.[10] The diverse aesthetic sensations generated by the sweeping occupation events of a decade ago (Chapter 9), or the urban protest actions against white supremacy following the police murder of George Floyd (Chapter 12), do not merely involve putting artistic forms to use for political movements; they have instead come to be understood in their own right 'as both a political and an aesthetic entity', explains Julia Ramírez-Blanco with reference to the Occupy Movement – an observation echoed and amplified by Yates McKee, who proposes that OWS was itself a socially engaged work of art.[11]

This burst of academic attention also appears to disregard, if not up-end, the well-known caution of Walter Benjamin, who in 1934 argued that treating politics aesthetically was the methodology of fascism – a project initially proposed by the Italian Futurists and then executed by Mussolini, in a spectacle of colonial military violence against Ethiopia.[12] Benjamin famously countered that a historical materialist responds to fascism by politicizing art, thus demystifying the cold-hearted property relations, class antagonisms and the hidden barbarity concealed within high culture. If Benjamin's heedful anti-fascist thesis has indeed become inverted of late, it is an inversion made in the name of progressive political change, and the mutation is attributable to a phenomenon that was only in its infancy during his day. What the philosopher glimpsed in its embryonic stage, and what the Situationists sought to confront decades later, is the full-on aestheticization of the social itself. By now it unfolds everywhere, including inside the disciplinary cubicles of the workplace and classroom, within the home (if one has a home), but also in the affective spaces between us, and even in our minds, and our sleep, as new advertising technology is capable of encroaching on or invading our unconscious dream-lives.[13] As Boris Groys observes, 'the modern subject now has a new obligation: the obligation to self-design, an aesthetic presentation as ethical subject.'[14] Or as John Roberts puts it, 'in this present stage of mass machinization of immaterial labor, the reproduction/production cycle takes on a biopolitical character, in which the subject gives over his or her whole being to the waking part of this cycle'.[15] More than just a spectacle, it is our contemporary reality, or better yet, our shared unreality.

BARE ART

At last, we encounter the missing determinant for the recent explosion of art activism. It is not the exceptional privileges some still grant high culture that make this proliferation possible, but instead art's earthbound plummet into an everyday reality, wholly saturated with capital from megadevelopers and petroleum industry oligarchs, and capable of serving as a tax shelter, or mutual fund investment, or a cloak no longer even concealing real estate, debt and war profiteering. We have seen this fall from grace around the globe where criticism of the police or the government, including, in some cases, simply tweeting or making photographic or artistic representations of state abuse, has become a seriously punishable crime. A recent Russian law even applies the stigma of 'foreign agent' to any critic of the state who has ever received international support, such as a grant or award. Until recently, the statute was mainly applied to journalists and NGOs, but that first began to change when the artist Darya Apakhonchich performed a flamboyantly costumed street performance entitled *Vulva Ballet*, leading the St Petersburg-based feminist to be officially categorized as a foreign agent and 'national security threat'.[16] Pussy Riot and other activist artists soon suffered the same labeling fate, and with the war against Ukraine such dissent becomes a potentially long-term jailable offense. But even in the allegedly liberal democratic UK, a measure now winding its way through Parliament seeks to make noisy and disruptive public protests unlawful. If passed, the *Police, Crime, Sentencing and Courts Bill* could criminalize the activism of Extinction Rebellion, Black Lives Matter and many other socially engaged artists.

If art is now fully consistent with the ultra-spectacularized, yet utterly mundane visual and sensual excess of our time, it is a result of our society's fundamental addiction to the transformation of real events, large and small, into aesthetic consumables, from the viral videos of dying Syrian resistance fighters to a tsunami pounding a nuclear reactor in Japan, to American police officers murdering young Black people. All such content takes its place alongside online video clips of dancing puppies and cats, and more cats and puppies. Therefore, in all its relentless repetitiveness, the total aestheticization of everything is not just with us; it already *is* us. So comprehensive does this process appear to be that it might best be described as capitalist hegemony turned into a consummate design project, one that has incorporated even avant-garde experimentation and the imagined end of capitalism into the omnipresent menu of lifestyle-brand options. Is it any surprise, therefore, that art appears to be engaged in either direct forms of activism, or staging a clean get away? As theorist Stephen Wright proposes, art is scaling itself up to 1:1 in scale with life, seeking an escape into the everyday without a trace.[17] And perhaps both responses are actually connected?

Essentially, agreeing with Peter Bürger's famous critique that postwar artists normalized the early avant-garde's radical rejection of autonomy and desire to merge art with everyday life, Wright's 1:1 concept goes further by envisioning art's complete disappearing act, leaving no clues as to its departure, not even a Cheshire cat grin.[18] Is it possible that activism is now one of these artistic getaway tunnels? If the answer is yes, then it is also little wonder that protest activism has been gaining popularity among contemporary artists, for under current circumstances, activism seems to provide the only passageway out of our conundrum, even if taking this escape route means that the artist metamorphoses into an activist and the activist into an artist (and honestly, isn't that the least of our concerns now?).

And yet, as this book attests, art has been trying to exit from itself for a very long time. Even before the Situationists, Tucumán Arde, Conceptualism and the post-1968 collectives like AMCC and PAD/D, or the cyber-practices of tactical media and the anonymous public interventions of Craftivists and Black Lives Matter, the desire by artists to find a magic egress out of the embrace of capitalism, the bourgeoisie, the state, the church and the reach of oligarchs goes back further than the early avant-garde. But what none of these escape artists ever anticipated was their success, because far from vanishing as Wright proposes, or being dismissed as a bit of Marxist vaporware as Jacques Rancière suggests, or placed under erasure as Marc James Léger insists, or transmuting into Stalinism as Groys theorizes, or simply failing in Peter Bürger's terms, we must consider that the avant-garde, in conjunction with neoliberal capitalism, has at long last brought about the merging of art into life. Only, what should be a beautiful story of victory is taking place within a reality far removed from the exhilarating anti-bourgeois ideals of early-20th-century socialism or modernism. In which case, what haunts this newfangled consumer communism with tiny 'c' is the quandary of the *unpresent*.

In the words of the late Mark Fisher, we exist in a state of horizonless capitalist realism, where repetition and doubling dominate our sense of time.[19] But perhaps we have actually exceeded even Fisher's grim assessment, especially since 2016, and now with the return of war to Europe? Is it possible that we no longer find ourselves in a merely temporary detour from the normal, but instead occupying an uncanny time that I will describe as the *unpresent*: a condition of social calamity that does not even (falsely) promise a return to business as usual, and in which even the memory of better, more just economic, political or historical alternatives fades away. For example, during the COVID-19 pandemic, the marketplace continued to demand that we continue to labor as before, from 'home', via Zoom. Yet, this compulsory operation soon began to feel like a purely disciplinary or punitive exercise, as if the system was more obsessed with 'spending' our time, and making sure that we could go on consuming, rather than with actually extracting value. Perhaps not surprisingly, since the pandemic struck, millions in the US have abandoned their existing jobs. The mass media dubs it the 'Great Resignation', as if this were the eerie 21st-century counterpart to Marcuse's 'Great Refusal' of the 1960s. But this time around, the withdrawal seems less like an explicitly political, countercultural gesture than a retreat to the interior of the problem itself, as if there were nowhere else to go but back to the *unpresent*.

The condition of the *unpresent* may also explain the vehement monumenticide actions that have toppled not only tributes to white supremacists but also sometimes abolitionists, as in Martinique, where locals tore down a statue to the French politician whose 1848 mandate ended slavery (for the second time) in the West Indies. Rightfully, locals wanted a monument to their resistance, to persons with dark skin, and not that of even a noble, liberal patriarch. But this unreality swings in the opposite direction as well. Consider the blatant necro-revival of past or moribund regimes of domination, including of course white supremacy, but also the attempted re-imposition of an authoritarian, neo-Tsarist empire onto the Ukrainian people (originally 1721–1917) by modern-day capitalist Russia. It is the impossibility of knowing how to interpret this strange uncanny present that makes it all the more intellectually and politically debilitating.

If there is a cure for the *unpresent,* it appears to takes two opposing forms, two escape routes: a regressive identification with a mythical ethno-purism, or an opposite desire to abolish all tainted cultural institutions associated with the colonial past and its centuries of barbarity. As theorist Paul B. Preciado states, 'All statues are a lie. All statues are made to one day be toppled.'[20] Or, as artist Chloë Bass puts it, with regard to the 'normative' policed spaces that we encounter and participate in, 'abolition no longer seems like such a far-flung idea'.[21] Contrarily, if once the slogan 'Workers of the world unite!' managed wonders in its day, argues theorist Blake Stimson, then today 'our leading prevailing myth, as dispiriting as it may be, is a renewed anti-democratic ethno-nationalism and its rising tool is Internet-fueled communitarianism'.[21] Ironically, the archaic elite outpost of Greenbergian formalist abstraction becomes almost like a refuge for the idealized universal human subject previously projected to emerge in the aftermath of post-capitalist emancipation. Almost, but not quite.

The abolitionist activism of today is therefore not at all the same as AWC's reformist institutional critique or AMCC's calls for a radical cultural politics in the late 1960s and 1970s respectively. For if the cure for our delirious *unpresent* is an end to its entire psycho-historical countenance and the civilization that goes with it, then we have arrived back at the beginning, with aims resembling those of the Situationists, and their total and 'all-encompassing critique' of the spectacle. We might also look to the declarations made by Argentine artist León Ferrari, whose 1968 manifesto, which inspired Tucumán Arde, stated:

> Art will be neither beauty nor novelty, art will be efficiency and disturbance. The work of art achieved will be one that,

> within the environment where the artist moves, has an impact equivalent in a way to that of a terrorist attack in a country that is liberating itself.[23]

Today, the 'environment where the artist moves' is everywhere. It is the same for the activist. And even if we could apply some type of Turing test to determine whether this or that phenomenon is activism or is art, given contemporary circumstances, its outcome would always wind up as a paradox.[24]

HAUNTOLOGIES

I started this book by comparing it to a particle accelerator searching for elusive dark matter practices of oppositional creativity. The search field turns out to be a fragmented and boisterous one, a phantom archive overflowing with interventions, experiments, repetitions, compromises, minor victories and outright failures. I end now by replacing the accelerator image with another, perhaps equally preposterous conceit. Consider this brief volume a hauntology, Jacques Derrida's term for an unsettled obligation emanating from either the past or the future, or both.[25] Of course, regardless of its origin, that which haunts us is summoned by the conditions of the present, which is truly its only possible home. But in our ghost story, what materializes is not a vague apparition or seductive nymph, it is instead a shiver within the very logic of familiar expectations.

As Kim Charnley observes, art activism is a glitch that nevertheless has palpable consequences, including the mutual causality of the artist as activist and the activist as artist. And one significant outcome of this coding error is the reassertion in unpredictable fashion of all those unfulfilled historical demands for autonomy, liberated creativity, and self-directed time and labor, now repurposed and writ large as a horizon of risk, uncertainty and promise. This glitch also exceeds the field of art itself; Lucy Lippard's Trojan Horse is on the loose. Which is to say that, as summarized by the theorist Kuba Szreder,

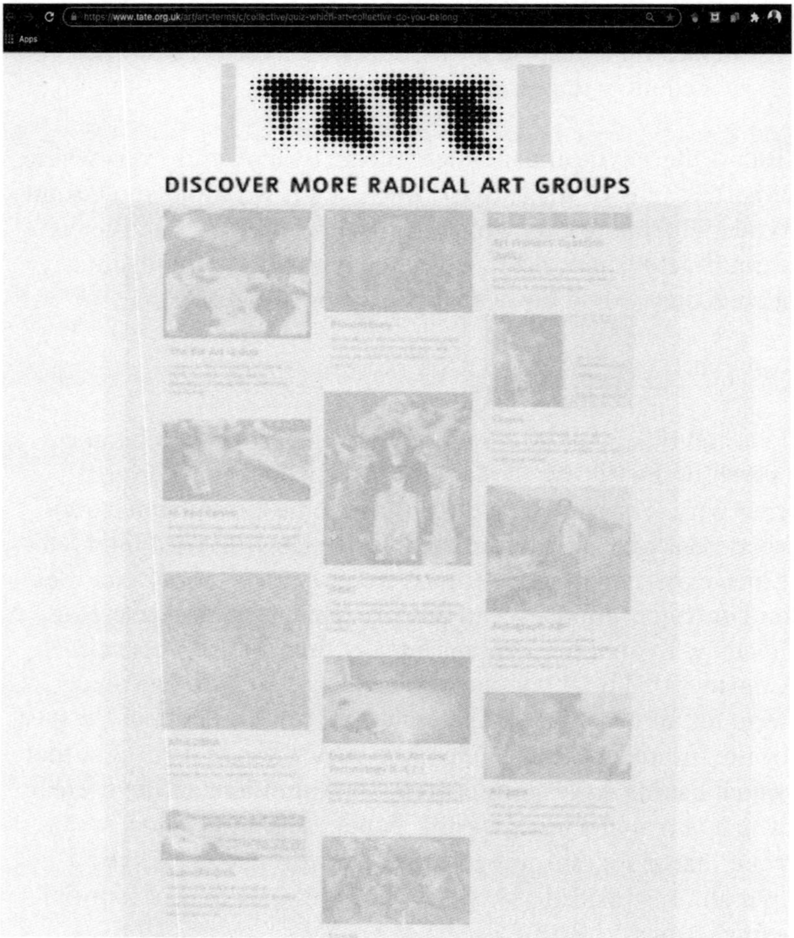

Fig.21 Tate's 'Which art collective do you belong to' online quiz page minus the radical art groups (see page 9), https://www.tate.org.uk/art/art-terms/c/collective/quiz-which-art-collective-do-you-belong.

activist aesthetics is 'repurposing social energies, reputations, ideas, and resources, gleaned from the global circulation of art, for the sake of [broader political] struggles'.[26] Clearly, the long march through everyday life now confronts a world that is anything but *everyday*, as a photograph tweeted less than two weeks into the 2022 invasion of Ukraine by Russia reveals (fig.20). In it we see a man in a welding outfit squatting beside what looks like a minimalist metal sculpture. The caption asserts that this is one of many artists working nonstop in northern Kyiv to create anti-tank barricades. I am not sure if the art of activism, and the activism of art, could have a more profound or sobering visual portrayal than this.

Poised between a desire to escape or to abolish a barbaric civilization with its concocted 'glorious white' past, or the militarized re-assertion of ethno-religious netherworlds, and the contrary need to embrace some concept of a better future, perhaps even reimagining the innovative state governance like that of the 1930s US New Deal or what contemporary French economist Thomas Piketty describes as socialism rethought – hardly radical, but perhaps realizable – we witness the contemporary art of activism and the activism of art conjoined into an indivisible contingency. Whether contemplating a prison break together, or a revolution, or merely the reconceptualization of existing institutions, theirs is a spacetime haunted by the elusive dream of historical agency and its unceasing hunger for total emancipation.

Notes

CHAPTER 1

1 Lucy R. Lippard, 'Trojan Horses: Activist Art and Power', in *Art after Modernism, Rethinking Representation*, Brian Wallis (ed.), The New Museum of Contemporary Art, New York, 1984, p.341.
2 Martha Rosler, 'The artistic mode of revolution: from gentrification to occupation', *Joy Forever: The Political Economy of Social Creativity*, MayFly Books, 2014, p.194.
3 'Quiz: Which art collective do you belong to?', Tate, published 17 June 2019, https://www.tate.org.uk/art/art-terms/c/collective/quiz-which-art-collective-do-you-belong.
4 On participatory and socially engaged art see G. Kester, *Conversation Pieces: Community and Communication in Modern Art*, University of California, Berkeley, 2004, and *The One and the Many: Contemporary Collaborative Art in a Global Context*, Duke, Durham NC, 2011; C. Bishop, *Artificial Hells: Participatory Art and the Politics of Spectatorship*, Verso, London, 2012; N. Bourriaud, *Relational Aesthetics*, Les Presse Du Reel, Dijon, 1998.
5 Walter Benjamin, 'The author as producer', in *Thinking Photography*, Palgrave, London, 1982, pp 15–31.
6 Cited in David Cottington, *The Avant-Garde: A Very Short Introduction*, Oxford University Press, Oxford, 2013, p.22.
7 Vladimir Lenin, 'Party Organization and Party Literature', in *Lenin on Literature and Art*, Wildside Press, 2008, p.22.
8 PAD/D newsletter, *1st issue*, February 1981, https://guernica.museoreinasofia.es/en/document/1st-issue-and-upfront.
9 I discuss Steyerl's project in 'NFT Fever: Is it Time for a Great Refusal 2.0?', *Electra* magazine, #14, 2021, https://networkcultures.org/moneylab/2021/11/03/gregory-sholette-on-nft-fever-is-it-time-for-a-great-refusal-2-0/.
10 Gregory Sholette, 'Questionnaire: Sholette', *October* 123, Winter 2008, pp 135–8, https://direct.mit.edu/octo/article/doi/10.1162/octo.2008.123.1.135/56160/Questionnaire-Sholette.
11 ibid., p.135.
12 'Power 100', *ArtReview*, 2020, https://artreview.com/power-100/. The trend continued in 2022, with a majority of collectives and non-white individuals ranked 2–20, except that the top influencer was the NFT.
13 Tom Seymour, 'Turner Prize 2021 with a "pub without permission"', *The Art Newspaper*, 1 December 2021, https://www.theartnewspaper.com/2021/12/01/northern-irish-activist-collective-wins-turner-prize-2021.

14 A selection of other relevant books since 2019 is found in Further Selected Reading, p.68.
15 Peter Weibel (ed.), *Global Activism: Art and Conflict in the 21st Century*, MIT Press, Cambridge, MA, 2015), book cover description; Boris Groys, 'On Art Activism', *e-flux* Journal #56, June 2014, pp 1–14, https://www.e-flux.com/journal/56/60343/on-art-activism/.
16 See list of relevant selected archives on p.169.
17 Latimer is specifically concerned with the reconstruction of feminist and queer histories, and I am extending her argument to include the missing archive of socially engaged artists and collectives. See Latimer, 'Improper Objects: Performing Queer/Feminist Art/History', in *Otherwise: Imagining Queer Feminist Art Histories*, Amelia Jones and Erin Silver (eds), Manchester University Press, Manchester, UK, 2016, p.93.
18 Antonio Gramsci, *Selections from the prison notebooks of Antonio Gramsci: 1929-1935*, International Publishers, New York, 1971, p.324.
19 Gregory Sholette, *Dark Matter: Art and Politics in the Age of Enterprise* Culture, Pluto Press, London, 2010.
20 Gogarty is making reference here to a phrase coined by literary critic Van Wyck Brooks, see Larne Abse Gogarty, *Usable Pasts: Social Practice and State Formation in American Art*, Brill, The Netherlands, 2022.

CHAPTER 2

1 Guy Debord, *Comments on the Society of the Spectacle*, Malcolm Imrie (trans.), vol.18, Verso, London and New York, 1990, https://monoskop.org/images/3/3b/Debord_Guy_Comments_on_the_Society_of_the_Spectacle_1990.pdf.
2 See Mikkel Bolt Rasmussen, *After the Great Refusal: Essays on Contemporary Art, Its Contradictions and Difficulties*, Zer0 Books, Winchester, 2018.
3 Sadie Plant, *The Most Radical Gesture: The Situationist International in a Postmodern Age*, Routledge, Milton Park, UK, 2002, p.3.
4 Karl Marx and Friedrich Engels, *The German Ideology*, 3rd ed., Progress Publishers, Moscow, 1976, pp 44–5.
5 Guy Debord, *Comments on Society of the Spectacle*, Verso, London, 1984, p.66.
6 'Address to the Revolutionaries of Algeria and of All Countries', in *Situationist International Anthology*, Ken Knabb (ed.), Bureau of Public Secrets, Berkeley, CA, 1981, p.190.
7 Guy Debord, 'The Situationists and the New Forms of Action in Politics and Art', in *Situationist International Anthology*, ibid., p.402.
8 Jacques Rancière, *The Politics of Aesthetics*, Bloomsbury Publishing, London, 2013.
9 Debord, 'The Situationists and the New Forms of Action in Politics and Art', op.cit., p.402.
10 Guy Debord, cited by Samuel Earle, 'The left's belated, and bittersweet, victory on climate change', *Aljazeera*, 15 October 2020, https://www.aljazeera.com/opinions/2020/10/15/the-lefts-belated-and-bittersweet-victory-on-climate-change.

11 Jeffrey Skoller, *Shadows, Specters, Shards: Making History in Avant-garde Film*, University of Minnesota Press, 2005, p.107. Skoller and Craig Baldwin carried out Situationist-inspired acts of visual repurposing in the 1980s, 'liberating' public billboards in the Bay Area.
12 U.N.E.F. Strasbourg, *On the Poverty of Student Life: A Consideration of Its Economic, Political, Psychological, Sexual, and Particularly Intellectual Aspects, and of a Modest Proposal for Its Remedy*, Strasbourg, 1966, http://library.nothingness.org/articles/SI/en/display/4.
13 Herbert Marcuse, *One-Dimensional Man: Studies in the Ideology of Advanced Industrial Society*, Beacon Press, 2nd ed.,1991, p.63.
14 Socialism with a human face was the slogan of Chairman Alexander Dubček's brief attempt at democratizing the Communist Party of Czechoslovakia, known as the Prague Spring in 1968.
15 U.N.E.F. Strasbourg, *Poverty of Student Life*, op.cit.
16 Antigoni Memou, *Photography and Social Movements: From the Globalisation of the Movement (1968) to the Movement Against Globalisation (2001)*, Manchester University Press, Manchester, UK, 2018, p.72.
17 Stevphen Shukaitis, *The* Composition *of Movements to Come: Aesthetics and Cultural Labour After the Avant-Garde*, Rowman & Littlefield, Lanham, MD, 2015, back cover book description.
18 Jelena Stojanovic, 'Internationaleries: Collectivism, the Grotesque, and Cold War Functionalism', in *Collectivism after Modernism: The Art of Social Imagination After 1945*, Blake Stimson and Gregory Sholette (eds), University of Minnesota Press, Minneapolis MN, 2007, p.36.
19 Sven Lütticken, 'Toward a Terrestrial', *e-flux* Journal #103, October 2019, https://www.e-flux.com/journal/103/291974/toward-a-terrestrial/.

CHAPTER 3

1 Lucy R. Lippard reflecting on her 1968 trip to Argentina with interviewer Michael Abatemarco, 'The road to Galisteo: Arts writer, critic, and activist Lucy Lippard', *Pasatiempo*, Santa Fe, 22 January 2021, https://www.santafenewmexican.com/pasatiempo/art/the-road-to-galisteo-arts-writer-critic-and-activist-lucy-lippard/article_30f25df4-335b-11eb-bc1e-3bd132721579.html.
2 Lucy R. Lippard, *Six Years: The Dematerialisation of the Art Object from 1966 to 1972*, University of California Press, Berkeley, 1997, p.43. Lippard erroneously attributed the entirety of Tucumán Arde to the Rosario Group, when they were just one constituent of the larger artists' coalition, see Ch.4.
3 This includes such writers on socially engaged art as Claire Bishop, Claudia Calirman, Julia Bryan-Wilson and Luis Camnitzer to Brian Holmes, Grant Kester, Yates McKee, John Roberts and Nato Thompson among others.
4 Ana Longoni and Mariano Mestman, *Del Di Tella a 'Tucuman Arde': Vanguardia artística y política en el 68 Argentino*, Eudeba Press, Buenos Aires, Argentina, 2010.
5 Mikkel Bolt Rasmussen, 'The Situationist International, Surrealism, and the difficult fusion of art and politics', *Oxford Art Journal* 27, no.3, 2004, pp 365–87.

6 Lippard, *Six Years*, op.cit., p.43.
7 Ana Longoni, 'Avant-Garde Argentinian Visual Artists Group, *Tucumán Burns*, 1968', *Mousse* 43, April 2014, p.18.
8 Longoni and Mestman, *Del Di Tella a 'Tucumán Arde': Vanguardia artística y política en el 68 Argentino*, trans. (unpublished), Microsoft Word file, 2004, p.156.
9 Lucy R. Lippard, *A Different War: Vietnam in Art*, The Real Comet Press, Seattle, 1990, p.13.
10 Longoni and Mestman, *Del Di Tella*, op.cit., p.16.
11 Ana Longoni, 'Is Tucumán still burning?', Marta Ines Merajver (trans.), *Sociedad (Buenos Aires)* 1, 2006, http://socialsciences.scielo.org/scielo.php?script=sci_arttext&pid=S0327-77122006000100003&lng=en&nrm=iso&tlng=en.
12 Gene Ray, 'Adorno, Brecht and Debord: Three Models for Resisting the Capitalist Art System', *The Nordic Journal of Aesthetics* 23, 5 June 2012, pp 44–5, https://voidnetwork.gr/2012/06/05/adorno-brecht-and-debord-three-models-for-resisting-the-capitalist-art-system-by-gene-ray/.

CHAPTER 4

1 Clement Greenberg, 'On Art and Politics', interview by Robert Burstow, *Frieze*, 6 September 1994, https://www.frieze.com/article/art-and-politics.
2 Lucy R. Lippard, 'The Art Workers' Coalition: Not a History', in *Get the Message? A Decade of Art for Social Change*, E.P. Dutton, New York, 1984, p.15.
3 Clement Greenberg, 'Modernist Painting', in *The Collected Essays and Criticism, Volume 4: Modernism with a Vengeance, 1957–1969*, John O'Brian (ed.), University of Chicago Press, Chicago, IL, 1995, p.86.
4 Hilton Kramer, 'Show of Political Prints at MoMA Echoes the Bad Taste of the 1920's', 'MoMA Print Show: The Same Old Artistic Stalinism', *New York Observer*, 22 February 1988, pp 1–9. Notably, the exhibition was also criticized by people on the left for having lamentably left out AIDS activist graphics. The catalog is available online at https://assets.moma.org/documents/moma_catalogue_1762_300296080.pdf.
5 The term 'advanced art' often serves as a euphemism for the most aesthetically sophisticated culture at any given time, and though contested, it still appears in the writings of theorists interested in socially engaged art including Grant Kester, Claire Bishop, John Roberts and David Beech among others.
6 John Hutton, 'Art and the Pain of Living: New York Political Art and the Protests of 1970', unpublished paper presented at the College Art Association Conference, Toronto, 25–28 February 1998.
7 See Andrew Hemingway, *Artists on the left: American artists and the Communist movement, 1926–1956*, Yale University Press, New Haven, CT, 2002.
8 American Association of Museums, *A Statistical Survey of Museums in the United States and Canada*, American Association of Museums, Washington, D.C., 1965, p.23.

9 See David Craven, *Poetics and Politics in the Art of Rudolf Baranik*, Humanities Press, 1997.
10 An excellent description of the collage and the entire event is found in Ch.4 of Matthew Winer Israel's book *Kill for Peace: American Artists Against the Vietnam War*, University of Texas Press, Austin, TX, 2013, https://erenow.net/ww/kill-for-peace-american-artists-against-the-vietnam-war/5.php.
11 Nadja Millner-Larsen, *Up Against the Real: Black Mask from Art to Action*, Ch.1 of the manuscript for her forthcoming book for University of Chicago Press. Also, as they did with so many admirers and detractors alike, Morea was denounced by the SI in a letter entitled, 'From the Situationist International to Ben Morea, 1967', *Enemies of Utopia*, posted 6 October 2010.
12 Numerous accounts of this document exist, including in Lippard, 'The Art Workers' Coalition', p.13, and Julia Bryan-Wilson, *Art Workers: Radical Practice in the Vietnam War Era*, University of California Press, Berkeley, 2011, p.237.
13 See *Art Workers*, ibid., Ch.3.
14 New York Artists' Strike press release, *c.*1970, Michael Goldberg papers, 1942–81, Archives of American Art, Smithsonian Institution, https://www.aaa.si.edu/collections/items/detail/new-york-artists-strike-press-release-9976.

CHAPTER 5

1 Pitchaya Sudbanthad, 'Emory Douglas', AIGA: The Professional Association for Design, 1 September 2015, https://epi.aiga.org/aiga/content/inspiration/aiga-medalist/2015-medalist-emory-douglas/.
2 Michael Hardt and Antonio Negri, *Multitude, War and Democracy in the Age of Empire,* Penguin, 2004, pp 189–90, and from *Empire,* Harvard University Press, Cambridge, MA, 2000, p.61.
3 Cristina Pratas Cruzeiro, 'Art with Revolution! Political mobilization in artistic practices between 1974 and 1977 in Portugal', *On the W@terfront*, vol.63, no.10, pp 3–35, 5 October 2021, p.22, https://doi.org/10.1344/waterfront2021.63.10.01.
4 Dara Greenwald and Josh MacPhee, *Signs of Change: Social Movement Cultures 1960s to Now*, AK Press and Exit Art, Stirling, UK & NYC, 2010, p.16.
5 Irene Wolt, 'The Story of Peace Press', Peace Press, updated 13 April 2005, http://peacepress.org/.
6 Mary Patten, *Revolution as an Eternal Dream: The Exemplary Failure of the Madame Binh Graphics Collective*, Half Letter Press, Chicago, 2011, p.29.
7 ibid., p.2.
8 See Lippard's comments at the start of Ch.6, p.59.

CHAPTER 6

1 Rasheed Araeen, *Art Beyond Art: Ecoaesthetics: A Manifesto for the 21st Century*, Third Text Publications, UK, 2010, p.78.
2 John A. Walker, *Left Shift: Radical Art in 1970s Britain*, IB Tauris, London, 2002, p.2.
3 The Catalog Committee of Artists Meeting for Cultural Change, an *anti*-catalog, 1977, front cover, http://www.darkmatterarchives.net/wp-content/uploads/2011/01/anticatalog.pdf.
4 Lippard, *Six Years*, op.cit., p.xxi.
5 Thomas Frank and Matt Weiland (eds), *Commodify Your Dissent: Salvos from the Baffler*, W.W. Norton & Company, New York, 1997.
6 *Finally Got the News*, directed by Stewart Bird, Rene Lichtman and Peter Gessner in association with the League of Revolutionary Black Workers, 1970, Icarus Films, 2003.
7 Max Horkheimer and Theodor W. Adorno's term for standardized and mass-produced popular culture in *Dialectic of Enlightenment*, Stanford University Press, Palo Alto, CA, 2020.
8 Artists Meeting for Cultural Change, an *anti*-catalog, front cover.
9 ibid., p.6.
10 Randy Kennedy, 'Contrarian Stays True to His Cred', *The New York Times*, 23 October 2014, https://www.nytimes.com/2014/10/24/arts/design/hans-haacke-gets-establishment-nod-of-approval.html.
11 As with many of the groups and projects discussed in this chapter, new scholarship is emerging to fill in gaps, such as Noni Stacey's 2021 book, *Photography of Protest and Community: The Radical Collectives of the 1970s*, Lund Humphries, though still much information exists in archives and online as primary material. For the Hackney Flashers see 'The Radical History of Hackney', Hackney Flashers, 21 June 2013, https://hackneyhistory.wordpress.com/2013/06/21/the-hackney-flashers/; and 'Work of a Women's Collective 1974–1980', Hackney Flashers, https://hackneyflashers.com/home/.
12 Lucy R. Lippard, 'Give and Take: Ideology in the Art of Suzanne Lacy and Jerry Kearns', in *Art & Ideology* The New Museum of Contemporary Art, New York, 1984, exh.cat., p.29, https://d2b8urneelikat.cloudfront.net/media/collectiveaccess/images/9/4/49236_ca_object_representations_media_9467_original.pdf.
13 See Claire Bishop, *Artificial Hells: Participatory Art and the Politics of Spectatorship*, Verso Books, London, 2012, especially Ch.9 on pedagogical projects, and Eszter Lázár, 'Educational Turn', Curatorial Dictionary', http://tranzit.org/curatorialdictionary/index.php/dictionary/educational-turn/.
14 *Black Phoenix* 2, Summer 1978, no.2, from back cover, http://www.darkmatterarchives.net/wp-content/uploads/2012/07/Black_Phoenix_2.complete.78.pdf.
15 Rubén Gallo, 'The Mexican Pentagon: Adventures in Collectivism during the 1970s', in *Collectivism after Modernism: The Art of Social Imagination after 1945*, Blake Stimson and Gregory Sholette (eds), University of Minnesota Press, Minneapolis, MN, 2007, pp 165–90.

16 Franklin Rosemont, 'Introduction', in André Breton, *What Is Surrealism*, Franklin Rosemont (ed.), Pathfinder Press, New York, 2004, p.21.
17 Alan Wallach, 'Rereading *An Anti-Catalog*: Radical Art History and the Decline of the Left', in *The Anti-Museum*, Mathieu Copeland and Balthazar Lovay (eds), Fri Art and Koenig Books, London, 2016, pp 451–60, https://primaryinformation.org/files/alan-wallach-on-an-anti-catalog-1998.pdf.

CHAPTER 7

1 Former executive vice president of Philip Morris, cited in Chin-tao Wu, *Privatising Culture: Corporate Art Intervention since the 1980s*, Verso, London/New York, 2002, p.125.
2 Brian Holmes, 'A Rising Tide of Contradiction: Museums in the Age of the Expanding Workfare State', *transversal texts,* April 2004, https://transversal.at/transversal/0504/holmes/en.
3 Temporary Services, *Group Work*, Printed Matter Books, 2007, p.88.
4 William H. Frey, 'Central City White Flight: Racial and Nonracial Causes', *American Sociological Review*, vol.44, no.3, 1979, pp 425–48, https://doi.org/10.2307/2094885; and Guy Debord, *The Society of the Spectacle,* Black & Red Press, 1977, section 174.
5 Michael Denning, *Culture in the Age of Three Worlds*, Verso, London, 2004, p.2.
6 Note here that in Italy, 1968's defeat did not really arrive until 1977 with the state repression of the so-called 'Years of Lead', Tony Negri, Paolo Virno, et al, 'Do You Remember Revolution?', in *Revolution Retrieved: Selected Writings on Marx, Keynes, Capitalist Crisis, and New Social Subjects 1967–83*, Ed Emery (trans.), Red Notes, London, 1988, https://libcom.org/library/do-you-remember-revolution.
7 Alexander Trocchi, 'A Revolutionary Proposal: Invisible Insurrection of a Million Minds', *Internationale Situationniste* #8, January 1963, https://www.cddc.vt.edu/sionline/si/invisible.html.
8 Luc Boltanski and Eve Chiapello, *The New Spirit of Capitalism*, Verso, London, 2005.
9 Lee Chun-Fung, 'How Is Art Political? The Political Construction in the Discourse of Art Activism in Hong Kong', *Journal of Contemporary Chinese Art*, vol.8, no.1, July 2021, pp 13–31, https://doi.org/10.1386/jcca_00035_1.
10 Nandini Bagchee, *Counter Institution: Activist Estates of the Lower East Side*, Fordham University Press, New York, 2018, p.2.
11 ibid., p.115.
12 Alan Moore and Marc H. Miller (eds), *ABC No Rio Dinero: The Story of a Lower East Side Art Gallery*, ABC No Rio with Collaborative Projects, New York, 1985, https://98bowery.com/return-to-the-bowery/abcnorio-the-book.
13 Richard Goldstein, 'The First Radical Art Show of the ''80s', *Village Voice*, 16 June 1980, p.1.

14 Group Material flyer from PAD/D Archive, *c*.1982; see also Moore and Miller, *ABC No Rio Dinero*, 1985, https://98bowery.com/return-to-the-bowery/abcnorio-related-groups
15 'Make Not Take', 1996 interview with Tim Rollins by Gregory Sholette, author's blog, https://gregsholette.tumblr.com/post/178288902435/make-not-take-tim-rollins-on-public-art.
16 Julie Ault, *Show and Tell: A Chronicle of Group Material*, Four Corner Books, London, 2010), pp 22–3.
17 Alan Moore, *Art Gangs: Protest and Counterculture in New York City*, Autonomedia, Brooklyn, 2011, p.114.
18 Gregory Sholette, 'A Collectography of PAD/D, a 1980s Activist Art Collective', *Routledge Companion to Art and Activism in the Twenty-First Century*, Mey-Yen Moriiuchi and Lesley Shipley (eds), Routledge (forthcoming).
19 8 PAD/D newsletter, 1st issue, February 1981, https://guernica.museoreinasofia.es/en/document/1st-issue-and-upfront.
20 '115 Years: The Manic Market of the Go Go '80s', Editors of *ArtNews*, 9 January 2018, https://www.artnews.com/art-news/news/115-years-manic-market-go-go-80s-9614/.
21 On Gran Fury see Avram Finkelstein, *After Silence: A History of AIDS through Its Images*, University of California Press, Berkeley, 2017; on DIVA TV see a video taped conversation with Gregg Bordowitz and Jean Carlomusto, Vimeo: https://vimeo.com/210630302.
22 Louise Owen '"Identity Correction": The Yes Men and acts of discursive "leverage"', *Performance Research Journal*, 2011, 16 (2), pp 28–36.

CHAPTER 8

1 Lawrence Lessig, *The Future of Ideas: The Fate of the Commons in a Connected World*, Vintage, London, 2002, p.9.
2 Geert Lovink, 'Tactical Media, the Second Decade', Institute of Network Cultures, 19 October 2005, https://networkcultures.org/geertlovink-archive/texts/tactical-media-the-second-decade/.
3 Francis Fukuyama, *The End of History and the Last Man*, Simon and Schuster, New York, 2006.
4 David Garcia and Geert Lovink, 'The ABC of Tactical Media', nettime, 16 May 1997, https://www.nettime.org/Lists-Archives/nettime-l-9705/msg00096.html.
5 Michel de Certeau, *The Practice of Everyday Life*, University of California Press, Berkeley, 1984, p.24.
6 Garcia and Lovink, op.cit.
7 ibid.
8 Gavin Grindon, 'Second-Wave Situationism?', *Fifth Estate* 380, Spring 2009, vol.11, pp 50–1; Yates Mckee, 'Tactical Media, Sustainability, and the Rise of the "New Green Revolution": From Neo-Situationism to Nongovernmental Politics', in 'Wither Tactical Media?', Gene Ray and Gregory Sholette (eds), special issue, *Third Text* 22, no.5, 2008, pp 629–38. See also McKee, 'Suspicious packages', *October* 117, Summer 2006, pp 99–121.

9 Garcia and Lovink, op.cit.
10 Michael Hardt and Antonio Negri, *Multitude: War and democracy in the age of empire*, Penguin, London, 2005.
11 Michael Denning, *Culture in the Age of Three Worlds*, Verso, London, 2004, p.2.
12 See Brian Holmes, 'Do-It-Yourself Geopolitics: Cartographies of Art in the World', in *Collectivism after Modernism*, Stimson and Sholette (eds), p.274.
13 Frank Bajak, 'Ukraine digital army brews cyberattacks, intel and infowar', ABC News, 4 March 2022, https://abcnews.go.com/Politics/wireStory/ukraine-cyber-official-attack-military-targets-83252854.
14 Josephine Bosma, RTMark interview, Nettime.org, 14 September 1998, https://www.nettime.org/Lists-Archives/nettime-l-9809/msg00034.html.
15 Michael Corris papers of the Art & Language New York group, Special Collections, Getty Research Institute, Los Angeles.
16 In 2001, Dow purchased Union Carbide, along with its decommissioned Bhopal plant.
17 McKenzie Wark, 'A hacker manifesto [version 4.0]', *Subsol:* http://subsol.c3.hu/subsol_2/contributors0/warktext. html.
18 Marina Naprushkina, 'Office for Anti-Propaganda', in *Entry Points: The Vera List Field Guide on Art and Social Justice No. 1*, Carin Kuoni and Chelsea Haines (eds), Duke University Press, Durham NC, 2016, pp 154–9; Carrie Lambert-Beatty, 'Make-Believe: Parafiction and Plausibility', *October* 129, 2009, pp 51–84.
19 Gretchen Coombs, 'See to Believe: The Center for Tactical Magic's Sleight of Hand', *Journal of Aesthetics & Culture* 6, no.1, 2014, pp 2–3.
20 'Taking Back the Plaque: The Art and Tactics of the Pocho Research Society,' *Home Magazine* #2, December 7, 2008: http://www.hijadela.net/wp-content/uploads/2019/12/lampertproximity.pdf.
21 See the documentary by David France, *The Death and Life of Marsha P. Johnson*, 2017, streaming on Netflix.
22 Cian Heasley, 'FBI FOIA Response Sheds New Light on Infamous Hacktivist Pentagon Incident', 27 October 2020, https://nscrutables.medium.com/fbi-foia-response-sheds-new-light-on-infamous-hacktivist-pentagon-incident-a44a318b4a46.

CHAPTER 9

1 David Graeber, *Direct Action: An Ethnography*, AK Press, Stirling, UK, 2009, p.418.
2 See Ch.8, note 22.
3 Frank Bures, 'The Fall of the Creative Class', *Belt Magazine*, 15 June 2012, https://beltmag.com/fall-of-the-creative-class/?gclid=Cj0KCQiAnKeCBhDPARIsAFDTLTJgO5ZNl5gxRIRRA4yQ_BAH0ZyfXrFdYr.
4 Marco Baravalle, 'Italian Blow-Up: Building Counter-Hegemonic Social Art Machines Against Reactionary Populism', *FIELD Journal* 12/13, Spring 2019, http://field-journal.com/issue-12/southern-eastern-europe/italian-blow-up-building-counter-hegemonic-social-art-machines-against-reactionary-populism.

5 'Liberate Tate Plans Mass Protest Over BP Sponsorship', *Artnet News*, '2 September 2014, https://news.artnet.com/art-world/liberate-tate-plans-mass-protest-over-bp-sponsorship-90479.
6 Human Rights Watch, 'United Arab Emirates: Events of 2019', World Report 2020, https://www.hrw.org/world-report/2020/country-chapters/united-arab-emirates.
7 See Naeem Mohaiemen, 'On Gulf Labor and Western Museums in the Middle East', Walker Art Center website, 7 December 2016, https://walkerart.org/magazine/gulf-labor-hans-haacke-naeem-mohaiemen; and Andrew Ross (ed.), *The Gulf: High Culture/Hard Labor*, OR Books, New York, 2015.
8 W.A.G.E.: Working Artists and the Greater Economy, https://wageforwork.com/home#top; see also Jillian Steinhauer, 'W.A.G.E. Calls Out Documenta for Not Paying Aritsts', *Hyperallergic*, 11 February 2013, https://hyperallergiccom/64958/w-a-g-e-calls-out-documenta-for-not-paying-artists/; for the Situationist slogan see May 1968 Graffiti on the website of the Bureau of Public Secrets: http://www.bopsecrets.org/CF/graffiti.htm.
9 'Report on the Economic Well-Being of U.S. Households in 2016 – May 2017', Board of Governors of the Federal Reserve System, 14 June 2017, https://www.federalreserve.gov/publications/2017-economic-well-being-of-us-households-in-2016-education-debt-loans.htm.

CHAPTER 10

1 Walter Benjamin, 'Theses on the Philosophy of History', in *Illuminations*, Hannah Arendt (ed.), Schocken Books, New York, 1969, pp 256–7.
2 Boris Groys, 'On Art Activism', *e-flux* Journal #56, June 2014, pp 1–14, https://www.e-flux.com/journal/56/60343/on-art-activism/.
3 Gregory Sholette, 'Coming Home to Roost: How a New Wave of Institutional Critique Confronts Our "Bare Art World"', *Free/Libre Technologies, Arts and the Commons*, Unconference proceedings, Phygital project, 9 April 2020, https://archive.org/details/unconference-proceedings-phygital.
4 The coalition included almost 40 groups including Chinatown Art Brigade, Queer Youth Power, NYC Solidarity with Palestine, Insurgent Poet's Society and the Illuminator; see DTP website, https://decolonizethisplace.org/9weeksofartinaction2.
5 'Arts Professionals Demand Moma Board Member Larry Fink Divest from Private Prisons', *Artforum*, 10 October 2019, https://www.artforum.com/news/arts-professionals-demand-moma-board-member-larry-fink-divest-from-prisons-81008.
6 Taylor Dafoe, 'Artist Michael Rakowitz Paused His Video...', *artnet* news, 13 January 2020, https://news.artnet.com/art-world/moma-ps1-michael-rakowitz-paused-video-protest-left-museum-turned-back-1751796.
7 Zaza Hlalethwa, '"We Must Recuperate Our Heritage': Congolese Activist Is Fined €5,000 for Trying to Seize an African Artefact from the Louvre',

Arts24, 21 December 2021, https://www.news24.com/arts/culture/we-must-recuperate-our-heritage-congolese-activist-is-fined-5000-for-trying-to-seize-an-african-artefact-from-the-louvre-20201221. For an impressively researched critique of colonialism in British museums see: Dan Hicks, *The Brutish Museums: The Benin Bronzes, Colonial Violence and Cultural Restitution,* Pluto Press, London, 2020.

8 Strike MoMA Working Group of the International Imagination of Anti-National Anti-Imperialist Feelings (IIAAF), section IV, point 8, *Strike MoMA: Framework and Terms for Struggle*, 23 March 2021, https://www.strikemoma.org/.

9 ibid., section I.

10 MTL's essay also offers an excellent historical overview of the Institutional Critique concept, 'From institutional Critique to institutional Liberation? A Decolonial Perspective on the Crises of Contemporary Art', MTL group, Cambridge, MA: *October* 165, Summer 2018, pp 192–227, https://monoskop.org/images/0/07/MTL_Collective_2018_From_Institutional_Critique_to_Institutional_Liberation.pdf.

11 Manifest Destiny is a 19th-century term asserting the God-given and therefore naturally inevitable dominance of white colonizers who were then expanded across the continent while displacing and replacing North American native peoples and Mexicans in what became Texas.

CHAPTER 11

1 De Certeau, *The Practice of Everyday Life*, p.xix.

2 Katharina Buchholz, 'Where Have Far-Right Parties Had Most Success in Europe?', *Statista*, 25 November 2019, https://www.statista.com/chart/20094/national-election-success-of-far-right-parties-europe/.

3 On utopian narratives from the populist political Right see Fredric Jameson's analysis of Walmart shoppers and political *ressentiment* in *An American Utopia: Dual Power and the Universal Army*, Verso Books, London, 2016, and *The Political Unconscious*, Cornell University Press, Ithaka, NY, 1981.

4 De Certeau, op.cit.

5 Oliver Ressler (ed.), *Barricading the Ice Sheets. Artists and Climate Action in the Age of Irreversible Decision*, Edition Camera Austria, Graz, 2020, excerpted https://camera-austria.at/en/presse/oliver-ressler-ed-barricading-the-ice-sheets-artists-and-climate-action-in-the-age-of-irreversible-decision/.

6 ibid.

7 Rena Rädle, 'Artistic Protest Practices in Serbia', *FIELD Journal* 12/13, Spring 2019, http://field-journal.com/issue-12/southern-eastern-europe/artistic-protest-practices-in-serbia.

8 ibid.

9 ibid.

10 '#SinMordaza', Proyectos, Colectivo Enmedio, 22 December 2014, https://enmedio.info/sinmordaza-una-accion-fotografica-contra-la-ley-de-proteccion-de-la-seguridad-ciudadana/.

11 'Athens, Greece: police evict squatted theatre Empros', *FreeDom* online journal, 19 May 2021, https://freedomnews.org.uk/2021/05/19/athens-greece-police-evict-squatted-theatre-empros/.
12 For the entire repertoire of women's strike symbols, see Kamila Wojtkiewicz, 'Symbole Strajku Kobiet', *Vogue Poland*, 11 April 2020, https://www.vogue.pl/a/symbole-strajku-kobiet; for more on contemporary art activism in Poland, see Archive of Public Protests, begun 2015, https://archiwumprotestow.pl/en/content/.
13 Center for Political Beauty, homepage, https://politicalbeauty.com/.
14 Philip Oltermann, 'Holocaust memorial replica stunt shines light on rightwing radicalism in Germany', *The Guardian*, 7 April 2019, https://www.theguardian.com/world/2019/apr/07/holocaust-memorial-replica-stunt-shines-light-on-rightwing-radicalism-in-germany.
15 Emma Anderson, 'German Artists Build "Holocaust Memorial" Outside Far-Right Politician's House', *Politico*, 22 November 2017, https://www.politico.eu/article/german-artists-build-holocaust-memorial-outside-far-right-politicians-house/. See also 'Holocaust Memorial in Bornhagen', Center for Political Beauty, https://politicalbeauty.com/memorial.html.
16 Center for Political Beauty, homepage. See also Karen van den Berg, 'From Protest to the Production of Social Relations: Socially Engaged Art and Activism in Germany since 2015', *FIELD Journal* 12/13, Spring 2019, http://field-journal.com/issue-12/northern-europe/from-protest-to-the-production-of-social-relations-socially-engaged-art-and-activism-in-germany-since-2015.
17 Bernadette Buckley, 'The Workshop of Filthy Creation: Or Do Not Be Alarmed, This Is Only a Test', *Review of International Studies* 35, no.4, October 2009, pp 835–57.
18 MTL Collective, 'MTL Reports: #GreatReturnMarch', *FIELD Journal* 12/13, Spring 2019, http://field-journal.com/issue-12/middle-east-africa/mtl-reports-greatreturnmarch.
19 The Lausan Collective cited from the webinar 'Art & Protest in Hong Kong', 18 November 2021, https://beinecke.library.yale.edu/event/art-protest-hong-kong [page is not found for security reasons].
20 Tania Bruguera, 'Reflexions on Useful Art', English translation, https://arts.berkeley.edu/wp-content/uploads/2015/03/Hibbert-Jones_Reflections_around_arts_utility.pdf.
21 'A Week in Havana at Tania Bruguera's INSTAR/Instituto de Artivismo Hannah Arendt', parts 1 & 2), Gregory Sholette's blog, 29 December 2017, https://gregsholette.tumblr.com/post/169079524365/a-week-in-havana-at-tania-brugueras-instar.

CHAPTER 12

1 Interview with Carrie Mae Weems by Dawoud Bey, *BOMB* magazine, 1 July 2009, https://bombmagazine.org/articles/carrie-mae-weems/.
2 Carlos Garrido Castellano, *Socially Engaged Art and Coloniality. Collective Creativity and the Materialization of Decolonial Futures*, SUNY Press, New York, 2021, p.270.

3 Nicholas Mirzoeff and Carl Pope, *The Appearance of Black Lives Matter*, Name Publications Inc., Switzerland, 2017, p.19.
4 ibid., p.21.
5 Imamu Amiri Baraka, 'Counter Statement to Whitney Ritz Broz', in Tom Lloyd, *Black Arts Notes*, originally self-published 1971, reproduced by Primary Information, Brooklyn, 2020, p.10.
6 Fred Moten, 'The Case of Blackness', *Criticism* 50, no.2, Spring 2008, p.187.
7 Nadine Bloch, 'The Art of #BlackLivesMatter,' 3 February 2015, OpenDemocracy, https://www.opendemocracy.net/en/transformation/art-of-blacklivesmatter/.

CHAPTER 13

1 Hito Steyerl, 'A Tank on a Pedestal: Museums in an Age of Planetary Civil War', *e-flux* Journal #70, February 2016, www.e-flux.com/journal/70/60543/a-tank-on-apedestal-museums-in-an-age-of-planetary-civil-war/.
2 Shellyne Rodriguez, 'How the Bronx was Branded', *The New Inquiry*, 12 December 2018, https://thenewinquiry.com/how-the-bronx-was-branded/.
3 Coco Fusco, 'The Art of Decolonization', presentation for FFT Düsseldorf, 10 June 2017, https://www.youtube.com/watch?v=4kWaY9q0zYI.
4 Kim Charnley, 'Art on the Brink: Dark Matter and Capitalist Crisis', unpublished essay, 29 June 2016.
5 Theorist Giorgio Agamben uses the term 'Bare Life' to describe a human being deprived of all socially constructed legal rights reduced to a state he calls *homo sacer*: a purely biological entity. What I am calling 'Bare Art' emerges when art's traditional autonomy, mystique and romance boils away, leaving the world of high culture stripped down and subsumed by the forces of modern capitalism and its political ideology. See my book *Delirium and Resistance: Activist Art and the Crisis of Capitalism*, Pluto Press, London, 2017.
6 Randy Martin, *Financialization of daily life*, Temple University Press, Philadelphia, 2002.
7 Dave Beech, *Art and value: Art's economic exceptionalism in classical, neoclassical and Marxist economics*, Brill, Leiden, The Netherlands, 2015.
8 See the special issue of Nonsite.org edited by Elise Archias, 'Contemporary Art and the PMC (Part One)', https://nonsite.org/issues/issue-37-contemporary-art-and-the-pmc-part-one/.
9 Aiden McGarry, Itir Erhart, Hande Eslen-Ziya, Olu Jenzen and Umut Korkut (eds), *The Aesthetics of Global Protest: Visual Culture and Communication*, Amsterdam University Press, Amsterdam, 2019, p.17.
10 ibid.
11 Julia Ramírez-Blanco, 'The Art of Occupation: Four Ways of Reading Protest Camps through the Lens of Art', in *Critical Cartography of Art and Visuality in the Global Age II: The Territories of the Contemporary*, Rafael Pinilla and Christina Grammatikopoulou (eds), Cambridge Scholars Publishing, Newcastle, UK, 2014, p.66; and Yates Mckee, *Strike Art: Contemporary Art and the Post-Occupy Condition*, Verso Books, London, 2016.

12 Walter Benjamin, op.cit.
13 Coors Brewing Company is working on a means of infiltrating dreams with commercials for its beer. See Adam Gabbatt, 'Nightmare Scenario: Alarm as Advertisers Seek to Plug into Our Dreams', *The Guardian*, 5 July 2021, https://www.theguardian.com/media/2021/jul/05/advertisers-targeted-dream-incubation.
14 Boris Groys, 'The obligation to self-design', *e-flux* Journal #00, November 2008, https://www.e-flux.com/journal/00/68457/the-obligation-to-self-design/.
15 John Roberts, *Revolutionary Time and the Avant-garde*, Verso Books, 2015, p.355.
16 Lucian Kim, 'Russia's 'Foreign Agent' Law Targets Journalists, Activists, Even Ordinary Citizens', *NPR*, 31 July 2021, https://www.npr.org/2021/07/31/1021804569/russias-foreign-agent-law-targets-journalists-activists-even-ordinary-citizens.
17 Stephen Wright, *Toward a Lexicon of Usership*, Van Abbemuseum, Eindhoven, 2013.
18 ibid.
19 Mark Fisher, *The Weird and the Eerie*, Watkins Media Limited, London, 2017, p.9.
20 Paul B. Preciado, 'When Statues Fall', *Artforum*, December 2020, https://www.artforum.com/print/202009/paul-b-preciado-84375.
21 Chloë Bass, 'Public Art as an Invitation towards Abolition', Finish Cultural Institute in New York, 2 July 2021, https://fciny.org/news/bass-public-art.
22 Blake Stimson, 'Infantile "Left-wing" Disorder: An Update', in *Contemporary Art and the PMC* [Professional Managerial Class], part one of a special NONsite.org online publication edited by Elise Archias, Issue #37, 2021, https://nonsite.org/infantile-left-wing-disorder-an-update/.
23 León Ferrari cited in Longoni and Mestman, op.cit., p.122.
24 Gregory Sholette, 'Do We Need a Turing Test for Activist Art in a Bare Art World?', *ASAP/Journal* 3, no.2, May 2018, pp 221–30.
25 Jacques Derrida, *Specters of Marx: The state of the debt, the work of mourning and the new international*, Routledge, 2012.
26 Kuba Szreder, *The ABC of the Projectareat: Living and Working in a Precarious Art World*, Manchester Press, Manchester, UK, 2021, p.201.

Appreciation

The shortcomings, omissions and suppositions in this study are entirely mine, though a number of individuals were completely essential for completing this study, including and above all my wife, Olga Kopenkina, who, while managing her career as a curator and writer, and teaching throughout the second COVID-19 lockdown in NYC, found the fortitude to assist my research, while remaining quarantined with me for over a year. And yes, we are still together. In addition, I thank my patient, perceptive and generous editors: Marcus Verhagen, Rochelle Roberts, Lucy Myers, Sarah Thorowgood and Clare Farrow – as well as the outstanding assistance of Jillian Steinhauer, Laura B. Thompson, A. Pollicino, Christopher Rowan and Maria Koutsouras who provided help with the preparation of the manuscript, that also benefited from indispensable feedback from Todd Ayoung, Marco Baravalle, Kim Charnley, Michael Corris, Raquel Ermida, Marc Fischer, Hans Haacke, Robby Herbst, Andrew Hemingway, Jerry Kearns, Grant Kester, Lucy R. Lippard, Ana Longoni, Josh MacPhee, Alan Moore, Kevin Repp, Lawrence Waldron. I also thank The Getty Foundation for making their archives accessible to me, and my ardent appreciation extends to the artists and art collectives who supplied images that grace this book, and the artistic activism that made this study possible in the first place.

Further reading

In addition to the many invaluable volumes and essays cited in the book's notes, I recommend additional recent publications to the reader, all dating from 2019 onwards, which are related to activist and socially engaged art.

Caleo, Ilenia, *Performing (Art) Institutions. Against the Autonomy of Aesthetics*, Gabriella Riccio (trans.), Institute of Radical Imagination, Naples, Italy, 2021.

Chto Delat and Free Home University, *When the Roots Start Moving. First Movement/To Navigate Backwards. Resonating with Zapatismo*, Archive Books, Berlin, 2021.

Crimp, Douglas, Alexander García Düttmann, Elsa Himmer, Ted Kerr, Elisabeth Lebovici and Nurja Ritter, *United by AIDS: An Anthology on Art in Response to HIV/AIDS*, Verlag Scheidegger & Spiess, Zürich, 2019.

Deepwell, Katy, *Feminist Art Activisms and Artivisms*, Valiz, Amsterdam, 2020.

Demos, T. J., Emily Eliza Scott and Subhankar Banerjee (eds), *The Routledge Companion to Contemporary Art, Visual Culture, and Climate Change*, Routledge, New York, 2021.

Downey, Anthony (ed.), *Michael Rakowitz: I'm good at love, I'm good at hate, it's in between I freeze,* Sternberg, Berlin, 2020.

Duncombe, Steve, and Steve Lambert, *The Art of Activism: Your All-Purpose Guide to Making the Impossible Possible*, OR Books, New York, 2021.

Guerrilla Girls, *Guerrilla Girls: The Art of Behaving Badly*, Chronicle Books, San Francisco, 2020.

Kester, Grant, *Beyond the Sovereign Self: Aesthetic Autonomy from the Avant-Garde to Socially Engaged Art*, Duke University Press, Durham NC, forthcoming.

Léger, Marc James (ed.), *The Idea of the Avant Garde Volume 2*, Books: Intellect, Bristol, 2021.

Leverette, Tru (ed.), *With Fists Raised: Radical Art, Contemporary Activism, and the Iconoclasm of the Black Arts Movement*, Oxford University Press, Oxford, 2021.

Lin, Jan, *Taking back the boulevard: Art, activism, and gentrification in Los Angeles*, NYU Press, New York, 2019.

Marchart, Oliver, *Conflictual Aesthetics: Artistic Activism and the Public Sphere*, Sternberg Press, Berlin, 2019.

McGovern, Alyce, *Craftivism and yarn bombing: A criminological exploration*, Springer Nature, Heidelberg, 2019.

Mesquita, Andre, Charles Esche (eds), *Arte e Ativismo antologia*, MASP, Lisbon, 2021.

Mollona, Massimiliano, *Art/Commons*, ZED Books, Bloomsbury Publishing, London/New York, 2021.

Pawlik, Joanna, *Remade in America: surrealist art, activism, and politics, 1940-1978*, University of California Press, Berkeley, 2021.

Reed, Thomas Vernon, *The Art of Protest: Culture and Activism from the Civil Rights Movement to the Present*, second edition, University of Minnesota Press, Minneapolis, MN, 2019.

Slifer, Shaun, *So Much to Be Angry About: Appalachian Movement Press and Radical DIY Publishing, 1969–1979*, West Virginia University Press, Morgantown WV, 2021.

Wang, Meiqin, *Socially Engaged Art in Contemporary China: Voices from Below*, Routledge Research in Art and Politics, 2019.

SELECTED ARCHIVES

Interference Archive: https://interferencearchive.org/

The Center for the Study of Political Graphics: https://www.politicalgraphics.org/ PAD/D archive at MoMA: https://www.moma.org/research-and-learning/library/faq#padd

Public Collectors (Marc Fischer's collection): http://www.publiccollectors.org/

All of Us or None poster collection: http://collections.museumca.org/?q=category/2011-schema/history/political-posters; Tamiment and Fales Library special collections at NYU: https://library.nyu.edu/locations/special-collections-center/

The New York Public Library's Gran Fury collection: https://digitalcollections.nypl.org/collections/gran-fury-collection#/?tab=navigation; Yale's Beinecke Rare Book & Manuscript Library: www.postwarcultureatbeinecke.org

The Women and Social Movements Library: https://alexanderstreet.com/products/women-and-social-movements-library

Dark Matter Archives: http://www.darkmatterarchives.net/

PAD/D newsletter UPFRONT collected online: http://www.darkmatterarchives.net/?page_id=72

Image credits

1 Screen shot, gsholette, December 3, 2020; 2 Courtesy Dread Scott; 3 courtesy of Luna Park; 4 courtesy of Etcétera; 5 photograph © Eugene Tulchin; 6 © See Red Women's Workshop; 7 Photograph by Maria Karras; 8 photograph 1983 © Andreas Sterzing, used with permission; 9 G. Sholette archives; 10 photograph courtesy of The Yes Men; 11 image courtesy the artists; 12 photograph courtesy Noah Fischer and Occupy Museums; 13 screen grab composites from online Facebook video, G. Sholette; 14 photograph used with permission of Gulf Labor Coalition; 15 Photograph Fotomoviento, www.fotomovimiento.org; 16 Courtesy of Center of Political Beauty; 17 image composite from online sources, G. Sholette; 18 screenshot of Twitter account by G. Sholette; 19 Robert Cohen/St. Louis Post-Dispatch; 20 courtesy Kosmos Tabir, Ukraine; 21 screenshot by G. Sholette.

Index

Note: italic page numbers indicate figures; page numbers followed by n indicate notes.

ABC No Rio art center (New York) 77, 79
ACT UP 88
Adorno, Theodor W. 41, 157 n.7
Afghanistan 19, 116, 127–8
Afro-Surrealism 23, 137
AIZ (magazine) 57
Alcántara, Luis Manuel Otero 130–131
Algeria 23, 26, 34
AMCC (Artists Meeting for Cultural Change) 54, 59, 63–4, 69–70, 82, 90–91, 146, 148
American Artists' Congress 42
American Indian Movement 53
Anderson, Michael *80*
Andre, Carl 61, 62
Anonymous 96
anti-catalog 63–4, 69, 70
anti-colonialism *see* colonialism/anti-colonialism
anti-fascism 13, 38, 42, 57, 69, 119
anti-gentrification street stencil (Anderson, 1984) *80*
anti-globalization campaigns 92, 98, 102
Anti-Imperialist Cultural Union 54, 89
anti-racism 32, 42, 67, 115
anti-Semitism *122*, 125
anti-war protests 17, 27–8, 32, 38, 43, 44–5, 56, 89
Anti-WW3 Internationalist Art Show 68
apartheid 65, 67
Araeen, Rasheed 59, 66–7
Arendt, Hannah 44
Argentina *see* Grupo de Artistas de Vangurdia
Art Space Sanctuary 110
art workers 61–2
Art Workers' Coalition *see* AWC
Artists Against Nuclear Madness 68
Artists' Call Against US Intervention in Central America 17, 81
Artists Meeting for Cultural Change *see* AMCC
Artists' Tower of Protest, The (Edwards/di Suvero, 1966) 44
Artists' Union 66
Artists and Writers Protest (1966–1967) *40*, 44, 46
ArtReview magazine *10*, 134
Arts & Labor 104, 105
Atelier Populaire (Paris) 28, 54
Autonomen squatters (West Berlin) 50
avant-garde 21–3, 26, 29, 35–6, 62, 68, 74–5, 94, 114, 125, 146
AWC (Art Workers' Coalition) 17, 39, 45, 46, 51, 54, 64, 78, 83, 90–91, 106, 109, 148

Baraka, Amiri (aka LeRoi Jones) 45, 82, 89, 137
Baranik, Rudolf 44
Basquiat, Jean-Michel 77
Beech, Dave 141
Belarus 19, 130
Benjamin, Walter 13, 69, 106, 111, 143–4
Berger, John 63
BFAMFAPHD 104
Bhopal disaster (1984) 91–2
Bichlbaum, Andy 91
Billy, Reverend 93
Bình, Nguyễn Thị *see* MBGC
Black Arts Movement 137
Black Audio Film Collective 9, 67
Black Emergency Cultural Coalition 46, 54
Black Liberation Army (BLA) 54

Black Lives Matter (BLM) 7, *10*, 17, 58, 121, 126, 131, 132–8, 145, 146
Black Mask 45, 91
Black Panthers 57, 77, 89, 137
Black Power movement 57
Boltanski, Luc 76
Bonanno, Mike 91
Bourgeois, Louise 56
Bowery in two inadequate descriptive systems (Rosler, 1974–1975) 64
BP (British Petroleum) 104
Brazil 116, 118
BreadTube 14
Brexit 116
Britain (UK) 12, 41, 50, 65, 66–7, 98
Brooklyn Museum (New York) 114
Brown, Michael 134, 138
Bruguera, Tania 130
Buenos Aires (Argentina) 32, *33*, 35
Bürger, Peter 146
Bush, George W. 15, *33*, 96

CAE (Critical Art Ensemble) 90, 94, 96, 100
California (US) 12, 53, 94–5, 154 n.11
see also Los Angeles
Cambodia 46
capitalism 21–7, 28, 29, 30, 31, 61, 74, 90, 98, 100, 145, 146
spectacular 23, 25, 43
see also consumerism; neoliberalism
Carbon Defense League 94
Carnival Knowledge 68
Castellano, Carlos Garrido 132
cell phones 57, 135, 137
Center for Art Activism 17
Center for Political Beauty (CPB) 7, *122*, 124–5, 126, 141
Center for Tactical Magic 93
Césaire, Aimé/Césaire, Suzanne 23, 137
CGT (Confederación General del Trabajo) 35
CHARAS/El Bohio Community Center 77
Charlottesville, Virginia 119, 120, 126
Charnley, Kim 139, 149
Chiapello, Eve 76
Chicago Surrealist Group 68, 82
Chicago Women's Graphics Collective 53
Chicanx movement 53, 95
Church of Stop Shopping 93
CISPES (Committee in Solidarity with the People of El Salvador) 82
civil rights movement 42, 43, 69
Cockrel, Kenneth 61–2
COLAB (Collaborative Projects) 77
Cold War 44, 84
Colectivo Enmedio 123–4
Collage of Indignation (Artists and Writers Protest, 1967) *40*, 45, 75
collectivism 11, 68–9
colonialism/anti-colonialism 12, 14, 23, 25, 67, 126, 162 n.11; and looting of artworks *107*, 111
Colston, Edward 135
Committed to Print exhibition (MoMA, 1988) 41, 155 n.4
Committee in Solidarity with the People of El Salvador (CISPES) 82
communism 23, 25, 41, 43
conceptual art 41, 54, 59–60, 64, 65, 82, 146
Constructivism 78, 89
consumerism 24, 26, 29, 38
Coombs, Gretchen 93
corporations 65, 84, *87*, 88, 91–2, 96, 100
counterculture 29, 37, 61, 74, 75, 79, 84
Courbet, Gustave 18, 135
COVID-19 pandemic 11, 105, 108, 119, 135, 147
CPB (Centre for Political Beauty) 7, *122*, 124–5, 126, 141
CPUSA (Communist Party USA) 41, 43
Craftism 92, 146
Critical Art Ensemble (CAE) 90, 94, 96, 100
Cuba 53, 54, 130–131
cultural activism 38, 68, 75, 76, 81, 88, 96, 100
Cultural Correspondence (journal) 82
culture jamming 30, 84, 92, 120
Czechoslovakia 27, 29, 154 n.14

da Costa, Beatriz 96
Dada 23, 34, 89
David, Jacques-Louis 18
Davis, Damon 134, *136*
de Certeau, Michel 88, 116, 121
de Gaulle, Charles 29
de Kooning, Elaine 42
Death and Taxes (PAD/D) 81
Debord, Guy 21, 23, 24, 26, 45, 71
Debtfair 104, 105, 110
DeCavara, Roy 43
decolonial movements 14, 76, 92, 95, 111–112, 121
Decolonise This Place (DTP) 7, 110, 112, 114
democracy 86, 100, 119, 126
Democratic Part Convention (Chicago) 28
Denning, Michael 74, 89
Derrida, Jacques 149
détournement 26–7, 30, 84, 88, 94, 120
di Suvero, Mark 44
digital technologies 14–15, 53, 57, 85, 89–90, 92; *see also* cell phones; Internet; tactical media
DIVA TV 84, 88
DIY activism 30, 52, 102, 77, 93
Diyabanza, Emery Mwazulu *107*, 111
documenta 8 exhibition (Kassel, Germany) 81
Domestic Labour and Visual Representation (Hackney Flashers, 1980) 66
Dominguez, Ricardo 96
Douglas, Emory 48, 57, 137
Dow Chemical 91–2
DTP (Decolonise This Place) 7, 110, 112, 114

École des Beaux-Arts (Paris) 28
EDT (Electronic Disturbance Theater) 90, 94, 96, 100
Edwards, Mel 44
Egypt 19, 101, 131
El Salvador 17, 81, 82
Elegies to the Spanish Republic (Motherwell, 1948–1967) 42
EMPROS (Athens theatre) 124
Engels, Friedrich 25
Etcétera *33*
Extinction Rebellion (XR) 121, 131, 145

Facebook 100, 102
fascism 115, 118, 143
FBI 82
feminism 42, 43, 64, 66, 68, 89, 145, 153 n.17
Ferguson, Missouri (US) 12, 120, 134, *136*
Ferrari, León 148–9
15–M 126
financial crash (2007-2009) 100–101, 104
Finisterra, Jude 91
Flag (Johns, 1969) 43
FloodNet 96
Florida, Richard 101
Floyd, George 114, 135, 143
Forensic Architecture 7, 110
France 23, 26, 50, *107*, 111; *see also* Situationist International
French Revolution 18
Fukuyama, Francis 86–8

GAAG (Guerrilla Art Action group) 17, 46, 106
gagging cow mural (Wojnarowicz, 1983) *72*
Garcia, David 86, 88, 89
Garner, Eric 132–4, *133*
Geometry of Resistance 128–9
Germany 7, 29, 48–50, 81, 94, *122*, 124–5
gilets jaunes 50
Giuliani, Rudolph 95
GLC (Gulf Labor Coalition) 20, 104, *113*
Gogarty, Larne Abse 19
Goldin, Nan 110
Golub, Leon 77
graffiti 35, 48, 51, 56, 77, 94, 129, 135
Gran Fury 66, 73, 84, 88
'Great Refusal' 27, 28, 30, 31, 83, 147
Greece 13, 124
Greenberg, Clement 39, 41
Greenbergian abstraction 44, 77, 82, 148
Greenspan, Jeff *97*
Greenwald, Dara 52

Group Material (GM) 69, 70, 77–9, 81–2, 84
Groys, Boris 17, 19, 106, 111, 144, 146
Grupo de Artistas de Vangurdia 31, 32–8, 61, 62
Grupo Proceso Pentágono 67
Guerrilla Art Action Group (GAAG) 17, 46, 106
Guerrilla Girls 66, 73, 84, 88, 110
Guggenheim Museum (New York) 64, 104, 106–8, 109, *113*, 123
GULF (Global Ultra Luxury Faction) 104, 112, *113*
Gulf Labor Coalition (GLC) 20, 104, *113*
Guston, Philip 42
Gwangju Uprising (South Korea) 48

Haacke, Hans 64–5, 109, 123
hacking/hacktivism 90, 92, 94, 96, 102–3, 130
Hackney Flashers 9, 66, 91
Hardt, Michael 51, 89
Harlem on My Mind exhibition (MoMA) 46
Hassani, Shamsia 127–8
hauntologies 149–51
Heresies Collective 68
Höcke, Björn *122*, 125
Holmes, Brian 71, 89, 93
Hong Kong 12, 19, 76, 101, 129–30
Howling Mob Society 94
Hungary 116, 118

Image War on the Pentagon (PAD/D) 81
In Mourning and in Rage (Lacy/Labowitz-Starus, 1977) *60*
Indignados, Los 126
Industrial Workers of the World (IWW/Wobblies) 68
Institute for Applied Autonomy 94
institutional critique 108–9, 111–112
Interference Archive 52
International Art Exhibition (Beirut, 1978) 67
Internet 14–15, 30, 57, 58, 83, 86, 89, 92, 98–100, 100, 102, 127, 134, 145, 148
Iran *128–9*, 131
Iraq 15, 92, 98
Italy 48, 75, 96, 102, 143, 158 n.6
IWW/Wobblies (Industrial Workers of the World) 68

Japan 48, 116
Jewish Museum (New York) 45
John Reed Clubs 39–41
Johnson, Martha P. 95
Jones, LeRoi *see* Baraka, Amiri
Jørgensen, Marianne 92
Journal of Aesthetics & Protest 142–3
JR (street artist) 132, *133*
Judd, Donald 42, 44

Kabul Knights 127–8
Kahlo, Frida 42
Kanders, Warren 109–110
Kearns, Jerry 71
Kent State University (Ohio) 46
Khouri, Kristine 67
kitsch 39, 55
Köpi (squatted housing project) 48–50
Krasner, Lee 44

labor unions *see* trade unions
Laboratory of Insurrectionary Imagination 93
Labowitz-Starus, Leslie *60*, 65–6
Lacy, Suzanne *60*, 65–6
Las Agencias 94
Latimer, Tirza True 18, 153 n.17
Lausan Collective 129–30
League of Revolutionary Black Workers 61
Leftist art 28, 37, 39–42, 44, 69
Léger, Fernand 42
Léger, Marc James 146
Lenin, Vladimir 13, 63–4
Lessig, Lawrence 86
libertarianism 23, 86, 118
Lippard, Lucy R. 9, 19, 32, 35, 36, 39, 59, 66, 149, 154 n.2
Longoni, Ana 34, 35, 37
Los Angeles (US) 53, 57, *60*, 65–6, 69, 120
Lotta Feminista 48
Lovink, Geert 86, 88, 89
Lukashenko, Alexander 130
Lütticken, Sven 30

McGarry, Aiden 142, 143
McKee, Yates 88, 142, 143
MacPhee, Josh *22*, 52
Madame Binh Graphics Collective (MBGC) 53–4
Marceuse, Herbert 27, 147
Marinetti, Filippo Tommaso 125
Márquez, Gabriel García 68
Marxism 23, 24, 28, 75, 78, 91, 146
May 19th Communist Organization 54
May 1968 uprisings 21, *22*, 25, 27–9, 35, 94
MBGC (Madame Binh Graphics Collective) 53–4, 106
Medu Art Ensemble (South Africa) 50
Memou, Antigoni 28
Ménil, René 127
Messer, Thomas 64
Mestman, Mariano 34, 37
#MeToo movement *10*, 17
MetroMobiltan (Haacke, 1985) 65
Metropolitan Museum of Art (New York) 46, 65
Mexico 27, 28, 29, 42, 67–8, 94, 90, 92–3, 96
military dictatorships 32, 35, 37, 81, 82
mockstitutions 92–5, 103
modernism 34, 37, 39, 47, 54, 59, 146
MoMA (Museum of Modern Art, New York) 17, 39–41, 45, 46, 51, 55, *99*, 105, 111–112
Monsanto 96, 100
monuments/memorials 7, 12, 112, 135, 147
Moten, Fred 137–8
Motherwell, Robert 42
MSUB (Museum of Contemporary Art, Belgrade) 123
MTL 112
Musée du Quai Branly (Paris) *107*, 111
Mussolini, Benito 143

nationalism 98, 115, 118, 119, 123, 124, 125, 148
Native American art 63
Neel, Alice 44
Negri, Antonio 51, 75, 89
neo-Situationism 88, 90–2, 93, 94, 96, 102, 114
neoliberalism 62, 64, 69, 73–6, 78, 86–8, 93, 96, 105, 116, 121, 123
New Communist Movement 89
New Deal 61, 151
New Left 23, 69, 82, 84, 89
New Masses (magazine) 41
New Museum (New York) 106
New York (US) 14, *22*, 31, 32, 36, 41, 45–6, 54, 57, 59, 63–4, 71, 76–7, 95, *97*, 120, 132–4; *see also* Group Material; *and see specific museums*
New York Artists' Strike against Racism, Sexism and War 46
New York Times 39, 44
Nixon, Richard 43, 46
non-fungible tokens (NFTs) 14–15, *16*, 141
North American Free Trade Agreement 92
nuclear weapons 48

Occupy Movement 7, 143
Occupy Museums *99*, 105, 110
OWS (Occupy Wall Street) 55, 90, 101–4, 120, 126, 143
October (MIT journal) 15–17
Office for Anti-Propaganda 93
oil industry 65, 104
Olek 103
Onganía, Juan Carlos 32
OWS (Occupy Wall Street) 55, 90, 101–4, 120, 126, 143
PAD/D (Political Art Documentation /Distribution) 14, 20, 41, 55, 69, 70, 77–8, 79–85, *80*, 82, 89, 146
Palestine 12, 67, 109, 112, 128–9
Paper Tiger Television (1981–present) 69
Paris Biennale (1977) 67, 68
Paris Commune (1871) 18, 29, 135
Paris uprisings (May 1968) 21, *22*, 25, 27–9
Patriot Act (US) 100
Patten, Mary 54
Peace Press 53
Pentecost, Claire 96
People's Choice exhibition (Group Material, 1981) 79
Peripheral Revolution 12

Picasso, Pablo 42, 51
Pignon-Ernest, Ernest 67
Plant, Sadie 23, 27
Pochx Research Society of Erased and Invisible Histories 95
Polak, Jenny 95
Poland 116, 118, 124
police 25, 27–8, 55, 66, 67, 82, 95, 114, *117*, 123, 145; *see also* BLM
Political Art Documentation /Distribution *see* PAD/D
Pollock, Jackson 83
Pop art 43, 53, 83
Popular Front 42
populism 116–18, 119, 126
Preciado, Paul B. 148
privatization *22*, 24, 101–2, 123
punk rock 30, 77
Pussy Riot 17, 145

Q. and babies? A. Yes, and babies (AWC, 1969) 51
QAnon 90
queer people/history 18, 95, 120, 153 n.17

racism 25, 65, 109, 118, 120, 121, 124, 125, 143
Rancière, Jacques 24–5, 30, 137, 146
Rasmussen, Mikkel, Bolt 34
Ray, Gene 38
Reagan, Ronald 17, 65, 81, 82
real estate 11, 64, 68, 76, 77, 114
Real Estate Show, The (COLAB, 1980) 68, 77
realism 39, 105, 130, 147
Reclaim the Streets 90
Red Herring (journal) 82, 91
refugees/asylum seekers 7, 109, 116
REPOhistory 20, 95
Ressler, Oliver 121–3
restoration activism 109–110, 111–112
reuse activism 94
Rhodes Must Fall 112
Rivera, Diego 42, 63–4, *99*
Roberts, John 144, 154 n.3, 155 n.5
Rockefeller, John D. 63
Rosemont, Penelope/Rosemont, Franklin 68
Rosler, Martha 8, 13, 64, 143
Royal Academy of Art (London) 15
RTMark *see* Yes Men
Russia 90, 98, 101, *140*, 144–5, 148, 151
Russian Constructivism 78

Saint-Simon, Henri de 13, 143
Salti, Rasha 67
Sanrizuka farmers 48
São Paulo (Brazil) 12
Saura, Antonio 67
Scott, Dread 15, *16*
SDS (Students for a Demographic Society) 68
See Red Women's Workshop *49*, 53
Semiotics of the Kitchen (Rosler, 1974–1975) 64
Serbia 7, 123
Servin, Jacques 91
Sex Pistols 30
Shakur, Assata 54
Shukaitis, Stevphen 29
Sierra, Santiago 125–6
Siqueiros, David Alfaro 42, 95
Sisters of Survival (1982–1986) 69
Situationist International (SI, 1957–1972) 8, 20, 21–31, 34, 38, 46, 62, 75, 141, 144; and avant-garde 21–3, 26, 29; and *détournement* 26–7, 30, 84, 88, 94, 120–121; and 'Great Refusal' 27, 28, 30, 31; and Grupo de Artistas de Vangurdia 35–6; influence/legacy of 30–31, 35–6, 45, 112; and May 1968 uprisings 21, *22*, 25, 27–9; and spectacular capitalism 21–7, 43, 74; *see also* neo-Situationism
Skoller, Jeffrey 26, 154 n.11
Smith, Adam 88
Snowdon, Edward *97*
social movements 38, 41, 43, 47, 48–58, 73, 82
social networks 127, 138
socialism 13, 24, 27, 35, 44, 53, 86, 151, 154 n.14
socialist realism 130
socially engaged art 12, 17, 19, 34, 43, 79–81

South Africa 50, 65, 112
Soviet Union (USSR) 24, 27, 62, 74
Spain 42, 94, 98, 101, *117*, 123–4, 26, 131
Spero, Nancy 44
Spit and Chew: Art and Culture (Latham) 41
squatting 48–50, 76, 89, 102, 124
Steyerl, Hito 15, 139
Strano Network 96
Strike MoMA 111–112
Students for a Demographic Society (SDS) 68
Suliman, Malina 127–8
surplus archive 126–7
Surrealism 23, 26, 34, 38, 68, 137
surveillance *22*, 82, 96, *97*, 98, 104
Survivaball (Yes Men) *87*
Syria 19, 101, 127, 145
Szreder, Kuba 149–51

tactical media (TM) 30, 85, 86–97
Tahrir Square (Cairo) 101, 131
Take Back the Streets 88
Tate museums 9–11, 104, *150*
terrorism 68, 96, 98–100, 125, 149
Thatcher, Margaret 65, 82
Third Text (journal) 67
Three Centuries of American Art (Whitney Museum, 1975) 63
TikTok 14
Times Square Show, The (New York, 1980) 77
Tlatelolco massacre (Mexico City) 28
Tokyo (Japan) 27, 48
trade unions 25, 27, 35, 41, 43, 50, 61, 106–8, 109
Trojan Horse (Lippard) 9, 19
Trump, Donald 116, 119
Tucumán Arde 32, 34, 35, 36, 37, 38, 46, 66, 146, 148, 154 n.2
Turkey 116, 127, 131
Twitter 102

Ukraine 12, 19, 90, *140*, 145, 148, 151
Ultra Red 90
Unbribables, The 7, 123
unemployment 73, 100, 101
United Farm Workers 53
United States (US) 24, 39–46, 64, 65–6, 67, 68–9, 71–3, 74, 98, 101; anti-war protests in *see* Vietnam War protests; attack on Capitol 119–120; civil rights movement in 42, 43, 69; Communist Party of (CPUSA) 41, 43; far right in 116, 118–121; and Iraq War 15, 92; social movements in 51, 53–5, 57; tactical media in *87*, 93–5; *see also* California; New York
United We Stand exhibition (Artists' Union, 1974) 66
unpresent 119, 146–8

Vietnam War protests 17, 27–8, 36, 37, 42, 43, 44, 45, 51

W.A.G.E. (Working Artists and the Greater Economy) 104
WAR (Women Artists in Revolution) 45–6
Warhol, Andy 43, 83
Wark, McKenzie 92
Weather Underground 54
Weibel, Peter 17, 19
white supremacy 12, 114, 135, 143, 147–8, 162 n.11
Whitney Museum (New York) 45, 46, 63, 81, 108, 109–110
Williams McCallister, Omolara 134
Wodiczko, Krysztof 88
women 29
Women Students and Artists for Black Art Liberation 45–6
Women's Day March poster (See Red Women's Workshop, 1975) *49*
women's rights/liberation 9, 48, 53, 118
Working Artists and the Greater Economy (W.A.G.E.) 104
Works Progress Administration 61
World War Three Illustrated 69
Wright, Stephen 145–6

Yes Men 66, 84, *87*, 91–2
Yomango 88, 94
Young Lords Organization 89

Zapatista uprising 90, 92–3, 96
Zuccotti Park (New York) 102, 103